Praise for Clyde Edgerton's
Papadaddy's Book for New Fathers

"Novelist Clyde Edgerton's eldest child is thirty—and his youngest is six. His advice book *Papadaddy's Book for New Fathers* is notably free of angst." —*Los Angeles Times*

"This slim gem offers laugh-out-loud advice on every page.... Edgerton is so, so funny. He captures the rainbows, cheap thrills, and irritating potholes of parenting with splendid understatement. Interspersed throughout, however, are solid statements that take the mystery out of parenting.... For lovers of Bill Cosby and Erma Bombeck and for ticklish parents everywhere. Fantastic stuff."
—Julianne J. Smith, *Library Journal* (starred review)

"With a healthy dose of humor, Edgerton covers everything from head lice to in-laws (not that the two have anything in common)." —Chantel O'Neal, *Garden & Gun*

"Not so much a guide as a brief, amusing tour through one man's lengthy sojourn in the World of Dad.... In addition to practical advice—'Install the car seat ahead of time'—Edgerton brings a sense of play that is often missing from the genre."
—Bo Emerson, *Atlanta Journal-Constitution*

"*Papadaddy's Book for New Fathers* is a slim volume, but chock full of the minutiae, the challenges, and the glories of child-rearing."
—Adrienne Johnson Martin, *Raleigh News & Observer*

"When I learned that Edgerton had just published a parenting guide, of all things, I expected to get a few laughs. What I could not have anticipated was that his *Papadaddy's Book for New Fathers* would make me a wiser and more relaxed father, too." —Allan Fallow, *AARP*

"Not just humor, Edgerton also talks about the ecstasy and worry that comes with seeing a baby for the first time. He writes about giving children limits and freedom. He writes about everything from dealing with lice to in-laws to the day of delivery."

—Dawn Baumgartner Vaughan, *Durham Herald-Sun*

"Refreshingly, a parenting advice book worth its salt."

—*Kirkus Reviews*

"Amid a slew of unsolicited advice-giving parenting books written by celebrities whose prose reads like a run-on drunken sound bite, Clyde Edgerton's new book, *Papadaddy's Book for New Fathers,* is a refreshing little tome of witty truths from a guy who has learned to keep his wits through three decades of parenting. This is not his first time at the rodeo— Edgerton's four kids range in age from six to thirty. It also helps that he's a member of the Fellowship of Southern Writers and knows a thing or two about crafting a sentence."

—Kim Cross, *Southern Living*

"A culmination of Edgerton's three decades' worth of wisdom for expectant and new dads."

—Paige Crutcher, *Publishers Weekly*

"A hoot....At an age when most guys are contemplating retirement and the easy chair, Edgerton...decided to start a new family. Three kids. (The author earned a Distinguished Flying Cross in the skies over Vietnam as a young man; suffice it to say he not only possesses the right stuff, he has far more raw courage than I do.) As an older dad, Edgerton pauses to note the advantages for others of his ilk. Unlike younger dads, for example, he actually knows what those funny words mean in Grimms' fairy tales, like scythe, hearth, anvil, and stockings....This one will be a perfect Father's Day present, regardless of Dad's age."

—Ben Steelman, *Wilmington Star-News*

Also by Clyde Edgerton

Raney

Walking Across Egypt

The Floatplane Notebooks

Killer Diller

In Memory of Junior

Redeye

Where Trouble Sleeps

Lunch at the Piccadilly

Solo: My Adventures in the Air

The Bible Salesman

The Night Train

Papadaddy's Book for New Fathers

Papadaddy's Book for New Fathers

Advice to Dads of All Ages

Clyde Edgerton

Drawings by
Daniel Wallace

LITTLE, BROWN AND COMPANY

NEW YORK · BOSTON · LONDON

Little, Brown and Company
Hachette Book Group
237 Park Avenue, New York, NY 10017
littlebrown.com

Originally published in hardcover by Little, Brown and Company, May 2013
First Little, Brown and Company paperback edition, May 2014

Little, Brown and Company is a division of Hachette Book Group, Inc.
The Little, Brown name and logo are trademarks of Hachette Book Group, Inc.

The publisher is not responsible for websites (or their content) that are not
owned by the publisher.

The Hachette Speakers Bureau provides a wide range of authors for speaking events.
To find out more, go to hachettespeakersbureau.com or call (866) 376-6591.

Library of Congress Cataloging-in-Publication Data
Edgerton, Clyde.
   Papadaddy's book for new fathers : advice to dads of all ages / Clyde Edgerton ;
drawings by Daniel Wallace. — 1st ed.
     p. cm.
   ISBN 978-0-316-05692-2 (HC) / 978-0-316-05693-9 (PB)
   1. Fatherhood.   I. Title.
   HQ756.E2434 2013
   791'37 — dc23   2012033851

10 9 8 7 6 5 4 3 2 1

RRD-C

Printed in the United States of America

for

Catherine,

Nathaniel,

Ridley,

and Truma

CONTENTS

PART THREE: **LATER ON**

PART FOUR: **THE LONG VIEW AND
AVOIDING FACTOR BAD**

Drawings by Daniel Wallace

AUTHOR'S NOTE 1

If you are an expectant father standing in a bookstore deciding whether or not to buy this book, quickly thumb through it and read what's in the boxes with a double asterisk and an exclamation point, **!, starting with the one about the car seat on page 13.

Then if you decide not to buy the book, put it back, go buy your wife some flowers, take them to her, and ask her for a date. Later on, if you feel a little apprehensive about a new baby on the way, come back to the bookstore and buy this book. Also, you might consider the following — to do as often as you can:

- Put toothpaste on your wife's toothbrush.
- Rub her shoulders for a minute or two.
- Make up the bed (assuming you don't).
- Make her a cup of coffee or tea, and breakfast.
- Rub her feet.

AUTHOR'S NOTE 2

Mothers and mothers-to-be, the cash register is up toward the front, I think.

．． ．

Back to you fathers and fathers-to-be. It's all mysteriously complicated—*fatherhood*. I'm hoping to give you practical advice (in the main). When I was much younger, I was the father of one child, and now I'm an older father of three small children—and my first child is now an adult. I will speak from experience, observation, and my imagination.

Papadaddy's Book for New Fathers

INTRODUCTION

I have a daughter, Catherine, aged thirty. I have a nine-year-old son, Nathaniel, a seven-year-old son, Ridley, and a six-year-old daughter, Truma. I'm sixty-eight. The age gap between the younger kids and me is not something I think about much, because I feel, physically, about like I did when I was forty—or at least I think I do. I think I...

I just forgot what we were talking about—age?

I do think about age, and as I write, if I have something to say to older dads (a growing population), I'll insert a short section labeled *C.O.D.—which means it's intended for the Considerably Older Dad. For example:

> ## *C.O.D.
> If you read tales from the Brothers Grimm and Hans Christian Andersen (your kids will probably love them), you'll be able to identify words in these stories that are not within the experience of younger fathers. Words like *hearth, anvil, harness, scythe, plough,* and *stockings.*

• • •

If you are a good person, you will probably be a good father. Try not to worry too much. If you don't feel apprehensive just before your first child arrives, you are abnormal. Though catastrophe doesn't come as often in childbirth as it did a few generations ago, we naturally fear it.

Then once our children are born, if we don't significantly interrupt the flow of childhood through them — that is, if we don't interrupt nourishment (physical and emotional) and play — and if the tone of our fathering is positive and we talk to our kids a lot, we'll probably do well.

A working definition of fathering might be this: fathering is the act of guiding a child to behave in ways that lead to the child's becoming a secure child *in full,* thus increasing his or her chances of being happy and fruitful as a young adult. This childhood season (spring), lived well, increases chances of a fruitful young adulthood (summer) and so on through fall and winter, each preparing for the next stage.

The early worldview of a child, the experience of seeing the world afresh, can be intoxicating for both child and father. When one of my aunts died about a year ago, this "new seeing" was demonstrated — if a bit morbidly.

Just before the funeral started, I entered the back of the church with our three little ones and my wife, Kristina. A cousin walked up and said, "The casket is still open if you want to view her." I looked at my children standing at my feet and staring up at me in bewilderment. They weren't familiar with what they'd just heard. What I next said to the kids, in large part because my mother took me to open-casket funerals about as often as she took me to the grocery store (a lot), was "Come on. Let's go."

At the casket, the kids lined up with their chins almost on the creamy-white silk lining. I stood behind them. Ridley, aged six, turned, looked up at me, and whispered, "Is she dead?"

I nodded yes.

My five-year-old, Truma, turned and whispered something to me.

I leaned in closer. "What?"

"Was she *always* dead?"

From a child's perspective, reasonable questions.

From an adult's perspective, odd questions.

Being a father can "unreason" your worldview, or at least make it very flexible, and that can create all sorts of fun and insights. It's sad that children's open-eyed wonder and sense of play begin to fade as they approach adolescence. One grand function of fathering is to keep the fading to a minimum.

By sometimes being playful and silly with my kids, I may help them hang on to some of the best parts of childhood, and thus reduce my chances of impeding that flow of healthy life through them.

I want this book to give you some good ideas, to take away some apprehension about that first year or so with your child, and to help you look forward to fatherhood. So I'll cover several important aspects of dealing with babies, toddlers, and little children in the first few parts of this book before jumping to "the long view" in a later section.

I will not usually break things down by months and stages (0–6 months, 6–18 months, etc.). In general, children know more than you think, and if you are wondering whether or not they are ready for a certain game, food, or task, try it and find out. If you're wondering about it, they're probably ready. My older daughter, Catherine, was ready to eat mashed potatoes before she could talk, and Nathaniel, my older son, was eating barbecued ribs *very* early on.

I will sometimes assume as I write that you have more than one child—but only one is sufficient for what we're about. That reminds me of the elderly woman living in a mountain hollow. She walked with a cousin into town at Christmas one year, observed a nativity scene, turned to her cousin, and said, "She had only the one, didn't she?"

If you were an only child, you remember the ups and downs of that. I was an only child, and I remember wishing I had a brother or sister. If you had a sibling or two, my guess is that you sometimes wished you were an only child.

As for more than one child, I'm reminded of the grandma who, at a family reunion, walked through a living room, past a couch with six or eight baby dolls lined up on it, and on into the kitchen. She said to a couple of women, "Whose children are them in there? They wouldn't even speak."

And, oh yes, there was the older nurse and the younger nurse with me in the emergency room one time. I'd brought in my five-year-old son, who'd stuck one of my hearing-aid batteries into his ear, way down into the canal, barely visible. It was finally removed with a little suction apparatus (and my hospital bill thus included a significant charge for "surgery"). But before the battery was removed, the younger nurse and I were discussing children. We laughed and talked for a while. The older nurse remained quiet, over in a corner, doing something.

The younger nurse said, "My aunt has five children."

Pause.

The older nurse looked over her shoulder and spoke: "I had two. If I'd had five, I'd a cut my throat."

The personal stories above are about women. It's not easy to find written stories about only babies and fathers. In America (and much of the rest of the world), the duty of child care has been cast to mere women — for all kinds of reasons.

Because we men have been physically stronger, and more arrogant, we've influenced much of the cool stuff of the world, like basing the definition of *courage* on what we do on battlefields rather than on the patience, or endurance, or tolerance necessary for a sometimes painful daily grind that includes small children. Manly courage sometimes pales when placed beside the womanly courage that is demonstrated in all sorts of places around the globe, day after day. Many women are alone as they care for children, without the readily available camaraderie or supplies that usually come to soldiers. Many of them die in the "line of duty."

As a consequence of the mother-baby, father-baby setup, many books and websites are dedicated to just Mom stuff. *Dr. Mom; Mother's Duties; Mother-Child Interactions; Your Baby and Your Breast; Breastfeeding with Ease* (keep reading)*; Letting the Left Breast Know What the Right Breast Is Doing; Breast to Mouth* (no, not that)*; Lymphatic Drainage and Your Cat; When One Is Bigger; Breastfeeding in the One-celled Organism; Breastfeeding in Church, Synagogue, Mosque, or Food Lion; When the Breast Won't Speak;* and finally, yourareolaandyou.com.

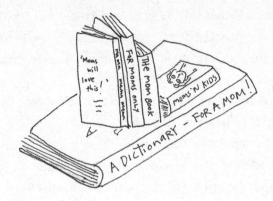

With this book, I aim to work toward evening things up.

Our fathering instincts, especially our ideas about "discipline," depend somewhat on the parenting we got as children.

I want to talk a little about my parents so you see where I'm coming from:

My mother usually stayed on top of her only child's activities, except when I was playing or hunting in the woods (with my own shotgun at age twelve, as was the custom in my place and time). (I don't suggest this.) She'd monitor me through a window when I was near the house.

She started taking piano lessons when I did at age seven; she was forty-seven.

She smothered me in some ways and pushed me out into the world in other ways. She took me on visits to nursing homes, jails (to see an uncle, and others), and she took me to see the electric chair when I was six. She was the dominant parent. She shaped me. And she (and my father) spanked, though not often. No, not each other. Me.

For a while, as an adult, I didn't like some of what I remembered of my mother's parenting style. That was when

I was beginning to try to be an intellectual. Now I think of her in positive ways almost every day. She was a good woman.

Though my father was relatively passive, I remember him in positive ways, too. He was gentle and kind—but a bit afraid of the world somehow. He was able to add long lists of numbers in his head as part of his job as a life-insurance salesman. Cautious. Very loyal to, and caring of, his blood family. He enthusiastically introduced me to quail hunting and baseball.

That I remember *how* they lived better than *what they said to me* is of course a cliché you read in parenting books—and is an important part of my message in this book. I also want to suggest that after they are gone, you will think often about your parents and what you learned from them directly and indirectly. If you did not grow up with your parents, you probably had parenting models you will come to think of often, negatively or positively.

While I was a child, my parents did not ask for my perspective about things, did not instruct me and then listen to my perspective without apparent judgment. That part was left to Uncle Bob, and in my twenties, to my cousin Barbara. If—for my younger children—I can be Uncle Bob; cousin Barbara; my daughter Catherine; my wife, Kristina; my mama and daddy, I think I'll do okay.

All eyes may now seem to be on your wife and her tummy, and nobody's throwing you any baby showers. Nobody's even thinking about you, it perhaps seems.

I'm thinking about you, although I'm not a professional parentologist.

When I started to write this book, my aim was not to tell you what to do, but to just describe some things I've been through. I wanted to be more descriptive than prescriptive. I've been both, and I hope you take from these pages only what might be useful and forgive the rest.

And if you are out of work in these hard times, you may have major concerns beyond the scope of this narrative. But I hope to convey that in spite of your hardships, your willingness to listen to and respect your children is an everlasting, priceless gift to the world.

PART ONE

GETTING READY

Preliminaries

CAR SEAT

> ### **!
>
> *Install the car seat ahead of time.*

A few weeks before the baby is born, go ahead and install the car seat. This could take six to eight hours. For safe installation, certain hooks are located out of sight down in the seat crack where you'd slide your hand if you were looking for something lost. If your car doesn't have these hooks, you are required by law to buy a different car.

One of your cousins or a brother or a sister-in-law will eventually inspect the installation of the seat and will get very upset because it's too loose or somehow not hooked up right, and they will call the authorities. This relative will be a vegetarian.

Another idea is to get a neighbor father who now has a baby to install your car seat under a bartering system. In exchange, consider offering to remodel his kitchen.

Children cannot sit in the front passenger seat of an

automobile until age twenty-four. Else the front-seat air bag will kill them. If the front air bag happens not to kill them, then the side air bag will try to.

Correction: after they are eighteen they can sit in the front seat if they face backwards.

If you decide to get your car seat installed at a fire station, a firefighter will give you a fire lecture. He will show you how to grab your baby and roll on it if it catches fire. A nurse will be on hand to tell you how to resuscitate a smothered baby. After the lecture, you are required to buy chain ladders to hang from each window of your house — first floor included. (The proceeds will go to the local Police Benevolent Association, and if you write down the wrong phone number, they'll stop trying to call you.)

IN-LAWS

If they are dead, your in-laws will probably not interfere with your fathering. But they *may*. Family norms tend to stay around for several generations — things like whether or not presents inside Christmas stockings are wrapped, whether or not shoes should be worn in the house. Whether or not Baby can stay up late at night, or watch television only one hour a day. In other words, even if your in-laws have passed on or live in Nova Scotia, they may still whisper into your wife's ear.

If your in-laws are alive and are reasonable people, you're probably okay. But if they seem occasionally unreasonable, then consider this: when talking to either of them, probably the mother-in-law, about real and potential baby problems, rely on the pronoun *I,* not the pronoun *you.* In other words, say something like "I don't think *I* want her to have that Popsicle while she's screaming," rather than "If *you* give her that Popsicle, I will kill you." This is something you'll have to practice beforehand — by yourself. Just look in the mirror and say things like:

"I can change the diaper."

"I'd like to hold her for a few minutes."

"I'd rather try it this way."

"Thank you, but I'm thinking that maybe I should..."

The words *uncomfortable* and *unable* might also be helpful. For example: "I'll be uncomfortable if she gets that Popsicle while she's screaming." Or "I'll be unable to agree that she go with you and Pee-Pa to Las Vegas. I'm really sorry." Don't say: "The hell you say."

If your spouse *and* her parents share many baby-raising ideas that you strongly disagree with, then I suggest you read my next book — due in about eighteen months. It will be called *Day to Day in the Dark Recesses of a Cave.*

YOUR WIFE

If your wife is pregnant, I'm glad you're reading this.

If your wife is *not* pregnant and the two of you are considering having a baby but don't get along well, and you're not too thick to see that, do what you will about counseling or divorce, but seriously consider not bringing another human being into your relationship until the two of you are feeling okay about each other. A bad relationship can mess up a child. Now, all of this puts me — as your fatherhood guide — on a slippery slope. Just about any generalization about parenting has exceptions, and you and your wife might be at each other's throats (sometimes clichés work well) but still end up with a happy, healthy child who grows into a happy, healthy adult. The variables relating to parenting are often too muddled to figure, and therein lies a problem with many parentologists who instruct with picky detail and high-mindedness.

Regardless of your relationship with your wife, this book is meant to help you — and thus, the two of you — get ready for a baby. While it's true that your wife may *not* be enthusiastic about motherhood, I'm suggesting that regardless of her enthusiasm you begin your preparation by telling *yourself* something like this:

"If necessary, I will *appear* to be confident in holding and talking to and caring for our baby until true confidence arrives — even if for whatever reason (including the "fathering" I got as a child) such behavior doesn't feel quite natural. And when the baby gets a little older, I will be silly with her, even if I've never been silly in my life. And I will ask her lots of questions and listen attentively to the answers, and I will try to provide reasonable limits to some of the more egregious elements of her behavior dating from prehistoric times, like a tendency to scream, bite, and hit."

Your wife probably will have planned well for the first few months of the baby's life. If your mother-in-law is around, she may also have planned well for the first few months of the baby's life, including stuff your wife missed. But there's a slim chance that your wife is in a daze, hasn't planned much, and in fact, may even seem in shock. Either way, you need to get a notebook and pen or a screen, and sit down with her and work out a few things. If she's a stay-at-home mom, you might say something like "Okay, I'll be able to help with cooking at these times during the first six weeks, with shopping for food through three months," etc. If you both work outside the home, or you're a stay-at-home dad, the language will be different, but it's still important to plan together. If a hurricane were on the horizon, you'd plan together. No, you're not going to get a hurricane — but at times you may find meaningful comparisons.

Let your wife know you're going to protect her from visitors she might not want to see. This may not seem important now, but it will later. When you see an unwelcome car drive up, you will walk out, meet the visitor, and say, "Mama and Baby would love to see you, but they're just getting to sleep. They really need sleep. I'm sure you understand." Something like that. Caleb, my cousin, on the birth of his and his wife Cindy's second child, put up a sign at the entrance to their driveway alongside their Beware of Dog sign. It read, Keep Out — This Means You. You'll be hearing more about Caleb and Cindy and their kids.

NONTRADITIONAL ARRANGEMENTS

There were probably no marriage vows in cave-people days. A norm (an unwritten rule for appropriate behavior, a definition we'll spend time on later) back then may well have been to kill your lover's lover. Later we invented marriage vows, and some murders have been avoided since then. And once we invented cars and they began running into each other, stop signs and then traffic lights came to be. We usually have legitimate needs that laws haven't yet recognized or are blocking.

In this book I'll be using the terms *fathering, mothering,* etc. I'm writing with specific cultural norms in mind:

1. You are about to be a father (again, maybe).

2. Your wife is a female and she is, or is about to be, the mother.

If you are in an arrangement different from this norm — for example, if you and/or your mate are gay, lesbian, bisexual, transgender, etc., along with being much like everybody else in tens of thousands of other ways — then I hope you'll be okay with my use of the traditional terms. You are at the forefront of a revolution that will see widespread changes in how the families are understood. New roles are allowing fresh insights into how families, old and new, can work toward good outcomes.

Because research on nontraditional family arrangements may be misleading or behind, I suggest this website: Father Involvement Research Alliance: fira.ca.

PETS

If you have a pet that you can never part with until the pet passes away, *skip this section.*

If you don't like your pet, and have no child attached to it, explain to your wife that the time needed for baby care makes pet care difficult. Then get rid of the pet in a humane and safe fashion.

If you are considering buying a pet and your wife just got pregnant, reconsider. Buy a stuffed animal instead. One that doesn't talk. In case you didn't know (though how could you miss it?), many stuffed animals talk these days. What they say is usually stupid or at best inane. If someone gives you one to give your child, consider taking out the battery and somehow disabling the battery compartment with a destructive instrument before your child sees it.

On the other hand, a talking stuffed toy may not bother you, and if that's a fact then you may have been one in an earlier life.

LETTERS TO BABY

Imagine—if you never got one—a letter written to you by your father before you were born (or soon after). I'll sprinkle throughout this book some that I wrote to my children from time to time.

. . . .

Dear Little One,

This morning your pregnant mom and I walked on the beach, and like we've been doing lately, we found something for you. Today it was a starfish. Several times lately we've picked up shells for you. We've been thinking about different names for you, but we haven't come up with anything yet. About four days ago, your mother got so excited she called me from her cell phone (they are pretty new) and said, "I couldn't wait to tell you. I felt the baby move!"

Love,

Daddy

. . . .

Nathaniel,

Last night I am sitting in the bathroom grading a paper while you (almost four) and Ridley (almost two) take your baths. There are about thirty plastic toys in the tub with you. The water is clear. Ridley says, "Uk-oh." I look and somebody has pooped in the tub. So I get you and Ridley out of the tub and commence to clean up the tub so I can put you back in and give you a fresh bath. I start in on the tub and toys and you say, "Papadaddy." I look. Ridley is peeing on the rug. I place him at the commode. He stops peeing. I go back to my cleaning. You say, "Papadaddy." I turn. Ridley is peeing on the sink cabinet.

Sometimes things are more fun for children than parents.

Love,

Daddy

Not Long Before
the Birth

ADVICE FROM BOOKS

An unsettling fact is that on the pages of parenting books you will find advice to *let* your child play with fire, to *not* let your child play with fire, to let your child sleep in the bed with you and your wife, to not do that, to let your child stay up as late as he wants, not stay up late, to spank your child (rare these days), not spank. Many books will claim the advice therein is based on "research." Some writers will try to make you feel guilty if you don't follow their research-based advice. Baby experts have feuds about all sorts of things—feuds about what to do with a crying baby at night, a crying baby in daytime, a mean baby, whether or not a baby can be mean, a sad baby, etc. There is a Method X, a Method Y, a Method G, for many parenting jobs, and you can easily become confused and frustrated—especially if you're used to following written advice.

Statistical research on dads suggests that fathers, on average, are older than they used to be and are also spending more time with their children. This is good. The bad news is that the older you are right now the less time you'll have with your children (or with yourself, in your present form).

So it's important to live healthily if you like being with your kids (and yourself). Some research also indicates that men with children live longer than men without them. Good news there, too. For us. Comments about older dads in the literature suggest that those really older — like me — seem to have more time to spend with kids and are more relaxed in their relationships with their young children. I'm not, however, suggesting you wait until you're sixty to have more children.

If you are not an expert in research methodology, it's very hard to know which studies to trust. Especially if the methodology is not described. Most everything you read will predict that if you're involved in your child's upbringing, the child will benefit greatly. But there's probably a website out there run by a small group of lumberjacks that will suggest that children who become lumberjacks will more likely have fun and get rich when they are older. The web has opened up a whole new landscape of research that isn't research, but opinion decorated with numbers and research language. Think about this. You could study the last days of a hundred men who died of heart attacks. Fifty died instantly and fifty after several days in bed. Conclusion: "From a study of a hundred men it's been proved that those who walked less in the last three days of their lives lived longer; therefore think twice before you go walking."

Another angle on this: there may be behaviors of your own parents that you dislike(d) but you find yourself practicing. For example, you may find yourself yelling to your kids: "Stop yelling!" It may be, without some serious thought, hard to stop doing that. Your children will tend to do what you do, sometimes when what you do contradicts what you ask them to do. A good bit of being a good father may be stuff you already know but nobody has suggested to you in advice books, on the web, or in research.

In the year 2200 we'll know far more about hormones, nutrition, baby sleep, brain functions, etc., than we do now, and people at that time will be scoffing at some of our baby-raising practices and policy in the same way we scoff at our ancestors for waiting so long to figure out the wheel, or for neglecting dental care.

While the reading on parenting is fascinating in its variance with itself, there are books and websites that give you, in addition to research findings, all sorts of helpful advice, like keeping your kids off TV before the age of two. (What about till twenty-two?) A couple of online sites set up by pediatricians and other health professionals are aap.org and health .nih.gov/category/ChildTeenHealth.

THE FATHERHOOD CULTURE

Neighborhood women, mothers-in-law, and grandmothers who, because they've been around so many uncreative, bland fathers—men who wouldn't pick up, change, or bathe a baby—will *fear* that you might be the same way, and they may spurn, ridicule, and ignore your attempts at parenting. What you *say* or *do* will probably not change them, so try to ignore the implications of their strategically placed bold digs. Just nod your head, smile, and say, "Yes, ma'am." (If they are vegetarian and/or from very large northern cities, they may ask you to not address them as "ma'am.")

In any type of parenting relationship, if you truly love your mate enough to stick out the marriage (or civil union or other arrangement)—according to statistics, roughly 50 percent of us in the United States do—you will want to relieve your mate of some, perhaps up to half, or more, of the hard work that comes with parenting. You will not want to be the stereotypical "helpless father." It's morally wrong to be that way.

You're now in relationships with your wife, parents, grandparents, uncles, aunts, siblings, friends, neighbors. Think about the relationships that are good, and why, and the ones that are bad, and why. You're about to be in a relationship with a child, and the tune and tone of that relationship will probably have similarities to some of your relationships with adults. A big difference is that with your child, you're dealing with an individual whose makeup, physical and mental, will be changing drastically, month by month, as you begin to influence that relationship. Your behavior with your child should thus change a good bit as that child matures.

Occasionally, as you've seen, I'll mention Caleb and Cindy, my cousins who have more conservative ideas about most things than I do. Caleb is a hunter, NFL fan, and NASCAR aficionado. He effectively parents his children, is tough and gentle, thick-skinned, capable, funny. And smart. One time in the supermarket, a smiling elderly blue-haired woman asked Caleb if the child in the basket were his.

He said, "Yes, ma'am."

She said, "Oh, you're *babysitting* today?"

He was very tired from parenting all day. "Yeah," he said, "and you must be *whoring* around the supermarket."

She reported him to the store manager, Erma Lewis... who was Caleb's cousin on Cindy's side of the family. Which probably helps explain why she called the police.

. . . .

A FEW DAYS OLD

Dear Nathaniel,

Mama's water seems to break at 2 a.m. approx., and then more surely at 6. We go to Dr.'s office at 8:30, and Dr. sends us to hospital. But we go back home and get stuff first. Nurse takes us to a room that's too cold. Thermostat has numbers so small you need magnifying glass.

Soon we're in a big birthing room. No contractions, so Pitocin is introduced after an IV is installed in your mama's hand. It takes a while to get needle in.

Finally the doc walks in. He looks a lot like Alfred Hitchcock. He takes little bitty steps and looks around like he doesn't know where he is. Looks at the machine, which by the way has all these cords and is what everybody looks at. They have a monitor outside as well as in the snack room (I find out when I go in to use the microwave...).

In comes a guy to replace a soap holder in the bathroom, pulling a cart with a tool chest the size of

a refrigerator. He sets in with an electric drill...
contractions slow, Pitocin increased, very painful
contractions. At about 3:30 or 4 p.m. we do epidural.
The nurse doing that is small, intense, with mask on
face, and your mama sits on bed with back to him,
and he says you need to get comfortable, bow your
back, etc., etc., and it's not going well. Your mama
says tell me what you're doing, and he's not at ease.
She finally changes positions and it goes well. Then
she has contractions for several hours with no pain,
or little pain. The doctor walks in, looks around.
"How's she doing [speaks very softly]?" He turns, goes
out. At 9 p.m. your mama is fully dilated. Dr. has felt
a couple of times, not much...so at 10 p.m. Mama
begins to push...10 p.m. to 12 a.m. — every 2 min.
she pushes, 10 sec. on, and then 10 off, and then 10
on. Your aunt Merritt counts to ten each time. Nurse
says when to push. We talk about if you'll be born
before midnight. Dr. seems to want to wait a bit. At
about 12 he puts a suction cup on your head. He says,
"There is a problem. He's not quite able to come
around the bend, so to speak, and so he needs some
help." Nurse holds tube connected to cup, to tell the
pressure, I guess (it'll pop loose when too much
pressure???). It does pop loose. Mama is pushing
mightily. The machine (green for contractions, red for
your mother's heart rate) has numbers, and it's got a
complicated program that the nurses try to figure
once in a while. Then it beeps and the second nurse
says, "Why is that thing beeping?" The machine

number on contractions is based-out at 18–25, and at 29 or so we know a contraction is coming.... When Mama is pushing, it goes way up, each time to 127 or so, which is a mighty push.

So at around 12:15 Dr. says if we don't get him out soon, we'll need to do something different. "We've bothered him enough this way," he says. So your mama pushes and pushes and out comes your head; then the doctor says, "Give the mightiest push of your life" and your mama does and you're OUT AND IN THE WORLD. I get a glimpse and the doc says, "Look at those eyes," and I see your eyes are wide open. Your aunt Katy is taking photos.... Your mama is very, very tired (we said it was like she was running a marathon, and while delivering, she'd make breathing sounds like "Hee, hee, hee who, hee hee hee who"). So they take you to next room to clean you up. I call your big sister in California; she hears you screaming—I put phone to your mouth. Your mama can't hold her arms up.

Within an hour we put you to your mother's breast and you start breast-feeding. You stay with us for a while in a new room, room 223. I sleep in a chair that night, and the nurses bring you to us when you are hungry.

You are in nursery a good bit of next two days, coming every once in a while to see Mama and Daddy, and we look at you. You sleep a lot, nurse, sleep, nurse, sleep. Cousins Barbara and Rosa Lee come to see you; David and Nancy McGirt come.

We stayed in the hospital Saturday and Saturday night, and then you and your mother came home on Sunday afternoon. There at home were you, your mother, your big sister, and me.

Then we went to Dr. next day. He wanted you to gain some weight. You were down from 8 lb., 10 oz. to 7 lb., 12 oz., so your mom and I worked hard and next day you were at 8 lb., and Dr. can't believe it.

You've been at home for four nights now, and you wake up and nurse in the night several times, and you look around when you are awake in the day. Your first visitor, Renee Dixon, our friend, came Sunday, and you also got your first letter from two boys next door, Edwin and John Hewitt West, and you also got your first telephone call, from Buddy Nordan, my good friend, and I'm going to try to record it onto the computer.

Right now, today, 11 a.m., you have gone with your mother and grandmother on a shopping trip.

May the Sun of Health and the Moon of Love watch over you all your days.

Love,
Daddy

. . . .

CHILDPROOFING

Childproofing homes started up after our species began using electricity and poison and glass to make the world an easier, prettier, and safer place to live in.

You will have no time to childproof the house (trust me) between the time the baby is born and the time it is old enough to aim and spray paint remover into its mouth. Here are some pointers:

1. Use insertable covers over electrical outlets. These look like plastic electric plugs that fit right up against the outlet cover. The idea is that babies will be unable to stick a fork in the outlet and shock themselves. Here's the deal: these insertable covers fit so tight against the outlet you can't get them out — *but the baby can.*

    The next best idea is to back a refrigerator up against each electrical outlet in your house.

2. Install baby-proof latches inside cabinet doors and drawers. These white prong-like plastic rods, each about the size of a cigarette, screw to the *inside* of a drawer or cabinet door and will keep them closed when latched to a latch device — unless you pass your finger inside the drawer or cabinet door after it's cracked about an inch and disengage the latch. When you close the cabinet door or the drawer, the latch engages again. Since you will not get used to these things until about the time you no longer need them, you might consider keeping them in place for your grandchildren — or grandparents. Remember that you won't need to childproof a drawer or a cabinet door unless something's in there you want to keep from the baby, or from the grandparents. Speaking of which, if you really want to have some fun with your

wife's grandparents, or maybe your own, then for their next birthdays give them a new remote control.

3. Set the temperature of your hot water heater no higher than 120°F to prevent scalding burns on your child (which reminds me, another way to have fun with grandparents is to give them Celsius thermometers). If you can find your hot water heater, there should be a dial on it for temperature setting. If you can't find your hot water heater, don't tell anybody. Or just ask your wife if she's seen something that looks like a round refrigerator.

4. Prevent poisonings by keeping household cleaners, chemicals, and medicines out of reach of children. You should *not* keep the chemicals behind cabinet doors with those child-safety cabinet door latches that we just talked about because about 70 percent of babies figure out the latches. Just put the poisons out of reach. But the child will learn to climb walls before walking — about the time you start climbing walls — and when he does start be sure he will not be able to open the poison or pharmaceutical containers. After age five a child can open those childproof caps or will find a hammer and crush the container. Write your Poison Control Center phone number on a piece of paper and hide it because you may need it. A sad fact is that your child may find this piece of paper and eat it.

5. Use stair gates. *Or,* better still, simply teach your toddler, as did Caleb and Cindy, to crawl up and down

stairs—as soon as he or she can crawl. You just
train him for three days to go up and down the
stairs on his knees while looking for a cracker you
have placed on every third step. The cracker will keep
him looking down, rather than trying to walk or
jump down the stairs. This can take a few days of
work but will be worth it. My wife and I moved to a
house with stairs when our baby girl was two. We
taught her to crawl up and down stairs, and then we
took down those stair gates. Think about it. If you do
install the gate, you want the child to know what to
do as soon as she opens the gate while you're at the
refrigerator or outside to get the mail or the
newspaper.

6. Install smoke and carbon monoxide detectors and fire
   extinguishers in the house. But know this: once
   walking, your child will use the fire extinguisher to
   put out something not on fire. And also count on
   this: at the worst time imaginable, probably in the
   middle of the night when you, your wife, and your
   child all have the flu, your smoke detector will emit a
   sudden sharp tweet. You will get a ladder and climb
   up to the detector, open it, and remove the nine-volt
   battery. After you've taken your flu medicine and
   gone back to bed, the alarm will tweet loudly again—
   even though it has no battery. At that time you will
   go outside to the electric circuit box and cut off
   electric power to the house. But in a few minutes the
   thing will [again] tweet loudly. At this point the best

thing to do is to make a torch of some kind and burn it up.

7. If you display a Christmas tree in your home, somehow wire it so it won't be pulled over as your child climbs it or holds on to a limb while walking to another room. If the wire is located where it will trip up elderly people, then remove chairs and tables from where the elderly will fall and put down some pillows on the floor.

8. Don't leave grapes out for your infant to find, eat, and choke on. Don't leave out fake grapes in their place. Don't leave out marbles. Or, if you're in a militia, hand grenades.

9. When cooking, use the back burners and turn pot handles toward the wall. This assumes your stove is backed against the wall.

10. To prevent drowning, empty all used water from bathtubs and pails, keep the door to the bathroom closed, and never leave your child alone near any container of water, especially those little plastic swimming pools. Those little plastic swimming pools, by the way, make great snow (or steep hill) sleds. They're not that easy to steer, though. Don't use them on hills heavily populated with trees.

11. If you must have a gun in the house, keep it in the attic and your bullets or shotgun shells in the basement or buried under the house where neither the child nor you can find them. If you confront a

robber, act confident and tell him that your brother is a cop and is on the way with pizza, and that he's always armed...and that the pizza will not be very good. Caleb keeps his guns in a walk-in safe that has a Jacuzzi.

Your wife may have most of the information above (and more) and plan to childproof the home after the baby becomes mobile. As mentioned above, this childproofing needs to be done *before the baby arrives*. Preferably by you.

(Caleb's father-in-law, Percy, childproofed his house so that *a child cannot get into his house.*)

> ****!**
>
> *The leading cause of death among children is accidents at home.*

BASSINET AND CRIB

For the first few months, before using the crib, you'll be using a bassinet. I'm suggesting you keep this in your and your wife's bedroom, assuming you use the same bedroom. Some experts declare that the baby should sleep with you, some say in another room. If you do go with the bassinet idea, most people buy expensive white wicker ones with little handles and a satin pillow and all that, or they inherit one. Caleb and Cindy realized that a little baby can't half see and couldn't care less, so why not use an ice cooler—with the top thrown away. Not the Styrofoam kind. The hard kind—like a Coleman.

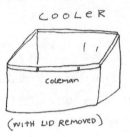

COOLER

Coleman

(WITH LID REMOVED)

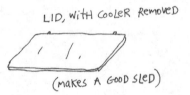

LID, WITH COOLER REMOVED

(MAKES A GOOD SLED)

When the baby is about three months old and you need a crib to replace the cooler (a crib is much bigger than a bassinet), you will be so sleep deprived you will not recognize your baby and will be falling down a lot.

**!

Assemble the crib before the baby is born.

The crib comes in a big cardboard box with staples so deep that you will need pliers and a flashlight to get these staples out. Most of the instructions for crib assembly come from foreign countries and say things like "Assemble Part B into upper part of Part B with plier." I assembled our crib in our living room over a number of days, and when at four a.m. on the last day of assembly—having just heard the morning paper slap onto the driveway—I started rolling the thing to the child's room, I found it *would not fit through the hall door.* Put the crib together *in the room where the baby will sleep.* Remember, for the first three months, the baby is in your bedroom in the cooler, or, if it's your style, in your bed with you and your wife, or perhaps with only you if your wife has retired to another part of the house.

While you're putting the crib together before the baby is born, your wife will probably be cleaning the house. Mother Nature tells her to do this like she tells trees to grow bark. Your wife, on hands and knees, will wash spots off base-boards with Q-tips. And when she asks you to do something, do it. In responding to her requests, don't ever use the word *logical.* Before my first son's birth, Kristina asked me to get a wire clothes hanger, put chewing gum on the tip end, and go deep inside the lint holder in our clothes dryer and get every speck of lint out so the clothes dryer would not catch fire and burn the house down on our first night home from the hospital. You know what I did? I did it. You know what I said? Nothing.

When the baby comes, it may be hard to plan and act ahead. You do not want to be putting in the car seat on the day you're to bring the baby home from the hospital. You do not want to put the crib together the day before it's needed. Let me say this again: *try to finish those tasks early.* When it's time to come home from the hospital or to move the baby from the master bedroom to another room, you want to be able to spend your time reassuring your wife, talking to her, and listening to her. She will need you close by, not away doing a task.

PREPARING FOR THE DAY OF BIRTH

After verifying pregnancy, your wife's doctor or midwife or a nurse will give you and your wife an expected date of delivery. The baby will not be born that day. This is a day you can plan to golf, fish, work in the shop, take in a movie, or read. The baby will come before or after, and if your wife's "water breaks," that will signal the imminent arrival.

The "water" is amniotic fluid from the breaking of the amniotic sac that holds the baby inside the womb, and most often the fluid will trickle, clear and odorless, instead of gush.

The water may not break until after contractions start or it may break twelve to twenty-four hours prior to contractions. If contractions are close together before the water breaks, take note. In any case, the baby is on the way. Put on your hat.

**!

***Know exactly where to take your wife
soon after her water breaks, or when instructed by
midwife, doctor, or nurse.***

The above may sound like an odd command, but there are similar names for hospitals and birthing centers. Paul Jones Memorial versus Paul Jones Med, Johnson County Hospital versus Johnson County Medical Center, and so on. You don't want to be birthing your own baby in the middle of the night on Interstate 40, having pulled off on exit 15 and then over onto that little gravel place where truckers sometimes park their trucks.

"Sweetie," you say to your wife, "there's a McDonald's .02 miles to the right. Want to head there — where there's a little more light?"

She will raise her head, look you in the eye, and say in a funny tone, *"McDonald's?!"*

Your wife will probably have prepared a bag of items to take with her to the birth. You will also need a small bag of goodies. I'd suggest your wife's favorite candy, and her favorite photo of you that you can tape to your baby's face because she's not going to be looking at you much for a few days after the birth. She'll be looking at the baby, in love.

You'll be kind of like that yourself. Experts say certain hormones will make you a little sobby and sentimental about the whole event. There's nothing much I can say here about what you should do during these first few days except give your wife anything she wants. She will have been through a big physical and emotional, perhaps spiritual, event. She will be elated but exhausted and she will need your attention. And you'll want to hold the baby and stare into his or her eyes.

PART TWO

BABY ARRIVAL AND FOLLOW-UP

The Birth

HOME BIRTH

Some people want a home birth. My parents and all my aunts and uncles were born at home because there were no options. As far as I know, none were the worse off for it. You'll use common sense and take advantage of choices, and if you've learned there is some disorder in the pregnancy, you will probably insist on a hospital birth or one with a doctor or midwife present.

TO THE HOSPITAL

When your wife is ready to go, she will tell you. Your job is then to call her doctor or midwife. When the recording says, "If you are a doctor or pharmacologist, press one," press one. You will get a recording that says if you are a father who pressed the wrong button, then you should press eight if your wife says she is ready. That recording will suggest that you stay at home until you can see the baby's head between your wife's legs. Don't heed that suggestion. The recording will also say that your wife, in that condition, should not operate a motor vehicle.

Get her to the right place with the directions you wrote down long ago. Stay calm, thus helping her to stay calm. Or pretend to stay calm.

Don't depend on an automobile GPS, because most models are programmed for a birth situation. This special programming sends you clockwise around and around a city block that is a quarter mile from the hospital.

NORMAL DELIVERY

Just before you and your wife enter the birthing room at the hospital, a nurse will hand your wife a gown with snaps and will say, "We use snaps so that if there's an emergency, the doctor can rip your gown off." This is a direct quote from just before the birth of my second child.

You do not have to worry about the birth part. That's taken care of by your spouse. You do need to worry about her every need. Encourage her to talk to you and realize that you can bring her comfort.

By the way, I'd suggest that you not video record the birth until after the birth part. I mean, this birth stuff is way beyond video—into mystery and...I don't think I can talk about it. In any case, you're probably not going to want to be doing the videotaping yourself. You want to be present in the world, in the action, not a part of the witnessing of it—that's what I think I mean. You want to be holding the baby right away, not holding an electronic gadget.

Ask the head nurse (the nurses have all the information you might need) about what's going to happen just after the birth. You can insist on being included. Most likely, in the minutes after the baby is born, nurses will gather around her on a table to check her out and get her breathing and so forth. Then they may wrap up and hand Baby to you to hand to Mother. But before all this, immediately after the birth, someone can hand you the scissors to cut the umbilical cord. A symbolic gesture you'll never forget. So get all of this straight with the head nurse prior to the birth. Your wife will be distracted and less interested in you than in other things. You don't want to be asking her what to do while she's giving birth.

If it's a Lamaze birth, you can be the one to hold your baby in a shallow pan of warm water, and stare into her eyes before she's wrapped up and handed to Mom. (I realized as I held my first daughter in warm water that the non-water-resistant watch I was wearing, a watch given to me by my father, was underwater along with my daughter (except for her face, of course). And there the watch died. The watch's last day was my daughter's first.

C-SECTION

Prior to the birth by C-section in an operating room, you will be standing beside your wife's head—which is poking through a hole in a hanging green curtain. Once the birth procedure starts, she'll be smiling, in spite of the burning smell from the searing of cut blood vessels in her stomach. When it's over, you will both be able to smile and cry and hold the baby. But the next day, when the pain comes on sure enough, she may say ugly things.

You will need to bring every ounce of comfort you can to

your wife. And lean on buddies, fathers, uncles, brothers, sisters, mothers, farmers, technicians, postal carriers, cafeteria workers, and others for all the good help you can get.

It may be that during the C-section you want to see the birth. I recommend going to the other side of that hanging green curtain if you've had experience as an observer in a medical tent during the Civil War and enjoyed it. My last child was birthed by C-section (they thought she was going to weigh over ten pounds—but she didn't, quite). I watched. The staff moved carts and things that were behind where I stood so that I'd have a place to fall if I fainted. It's not easy to say what a C-section looks like, and nobody prepared me, but if you want to know, I'm sure there's a video online. Okay, I just looked and found one sponsored by Target. It's a mess, man. I'm not sure you want to look. But I couldn't stand not to look at my wife's. I wanted to *see*. But your wife may want you right there with her...on the other side of that curtain, standing beside her, smiling down at her, making up something about what that odd odor is.

SEEING THE BABY

Remember this: the baby's head may not look exactly right just after the birth. That birth canal is relatively narrow, and your child's head, which you expect to be round, may be shaped more like a football. A small football...or hell, a large one. It will look normal in a day or two. Nobody told me about this, and one of my children's heads—the top only—was visible for a long time just prior to birth. The head was kind of stuck there and the part that was visible was not quite as wide as a fist, and that part ended up, after the birth, looking like a little pitcher's mound on the baby's head. The mound soon went away.

And listen, prepare for the unexpected, and ask questions if you don't feel right about something. For example, ask a nurse to explain those machines in the birthing room, because one will go off with a siren and a red rotating beacon. A nurse will walk in, walk up to it, and say, "OH MY GOD!" Unless you ask, you won't know that it's the room humidifier. Ask questions politely to anybody and everybody, about anything that puzzles you.

True or False? Holding a baby is like holding a sack of groceries?

YOU AND THE BABY

Hold the child in your lap, stare into her eyes, change her diaper, bathe her, dress her, and do this over and over and over. This human being is yours forever, or at least until, as Kahlil Gibran said something like, "You shoot it like a living arrow from a bow."

Usually, when you drop a baby, it bounces, cries, and is then okay. I've watched babies crawl over the far side of the bed, drop off the couch, stand up and fall backwards off the bed, fall off tables—and be unhurt. (I can't remember why one was crawling on a table. Probably dropped from the ceiling.)

. . . .

TWO WEEKS OLD

Ridley,

In about three days you'll be two weeks old. You're doing just fine in many ways. You're sleeping well for a tiny baby. Last night, for example, you woke up to feed at about 12:30 and again at about 4:30, and both times you went right back to sleep. We're putting some drops in your eyes three times a day because of a common tear duct problem. You don't cry unless something is very wrong. You look around, and you like to sleep.

Your big brother, Nathaniel, is three years old, and he likes to kiss your hand and look at you. He wrote a book before you got home from the hospital (with the help of Big Sister) that showed a rocket ship taking you to another planet.

Your mother has a sore breast, but I think it's getting better. She's crazy about you, and I am too. We're very lucky to have such a fine family.

I love you,

Daddy

. . . .

Pick the baby up and cradle him in your arms, fashioned into the shape of a new moon. Or you can hold him like a football. Like this: crook your arm as if you were a waiter with a towel over it. Turn your hand so the palm would catch falling rain. Put the baby facedown onto your arm with his chin in your palm and his legs straddling your arm near the elbow. You can also turn him around so that his head is at your elbow, facedown, and he's straddling your open hand. This method will impress people and is useful when the baby is not crying or fussy. Do not run on a football field like this.

Caleb owns an auto repair shop. The football carry is how he carried his first baby while he changed the points and plugs on his pickup. After doing that a few times, he put the baby down on the auto shop floor and then couldn't find him.

Know that after a week or two of handling Baby, you'll be comfortable holding him. (And here I'll venture a truth. While our culture is negligent in preparing girls for boy roles, and that is rightfully lamented, it's as drastically sad that boys aren't prepared for girl roles.)

A baby will be happy to hear you say anything; just make noise. I was once in a motel room. My black lab, Max, was curled up over in the corner. Max was an outside dog and had never been inside. There had been silence in the room for hours. I picked up the room phone and called somebody and said, "Hey, how you doing?" Max got up and came to me, wagging his tail. How was he to know I was not talking to him? One thing that will be fun is to speak to the baby in baby talk, saying something like "Gootchie, gootchie, goo, you little punkie-poo, you want to go with Cousin Caleb-poo to Las Vegas and get drunkie-poo and win some money-poo?" You know, that kind of thing. But maybe not, unless you're alone.

When my first child, Catherine, started making sounds, one of her nonsense words sounded like "Dewey," and so I started asking her, "Who's the father of American education?" and before she could talk, she would answer that question. It impressed some of my friends. After I got a little older and had more kids, I realized I was less excited about doing baby tricks. It might get old to your friends if you do it child after child.

NURSES

You'll probably find a nurse or two in the hospital who'll be extraordinarily helpful. You can somehow tell which ones are naturals with babies. While in the hospital, go to the nursery; get a nurse to show you how to change a diaper, and then let her watch you practice. If you get a talkative nurse, you can learn a lot of good stuff to take home with you. Ask all the questions you can think of.

Back Home

THE DRIVE HOME

On the drive home from the hospital, you will experience an odd combination of two feelings: a) extreme ecstasy and b) deep worry—about how the baby will keep breathing all night on that first night home, and how to keep, say, large rats away from it.

NOTE: rats have a hell of an easier time eating through wicker than through a cooler.

BABY SLEEP AND BABY CRYING PROBLEMS

There will be need for worry if your baby doesn't cry, and cry a lot during the first few months. You will be surprised at how quickly you jump from bed when Baby cries at night and from how far away you can hear a whimper. REMEMBER: the crying should ease up after three or four months. (More on that just below.)

People go crazy trying to get a baby to stop crying and to go to sleep. I've found myself, bent over, fingers in my ears, the top of my head pressed against a running clothes dryer—all to suppress sounds of a crying baby. I've found myself driving the baby around in his car seat at night trying to get him to hush up and go to sleep. One night I looked down to see that I'd forgotten to put on slacks and was driving around in my underwear.

See, those prehistoric hunter-gatherer babies who didn't cry didn't survive easily. Those who screamed, thrived. We inherited it.

Backing up a step, there is one important tidbit from the evolutionary info—a fact that may give you some perspective: the fetus, theoretically, should be in your wife's womb for twelve months, not nine. That's because a million or so years ago human heads started to get bigger. Women's pelvises, due to a standing posture, were getting smaller. So rather than stay in the womb for ten to twelve months and come out ready to dance, we now come out early, and those first three months out in the cold are difficult and frustrating. So we cry a lot. If you understand this, then you are in a good position to learn a secret about comforting a baby while reducing chances of crying.

A secret is to make a crying baby feel as if he's still in the womb—not always easy since he's breathing and much stronger than he was back in the amniotic fluid days. If the following Harvey Karp method to ease crying doesn't work on any of the first eight to ten times you try it, then forget it—or come up with a workable variation. If it does work, your wife will probably copy you. This 5 S's method comes from Karp's book *The Happiest Baby on the Block*: 1) Swaddle, 2) Stomach or side, 3) Shhhhh, 4) Swing, 5) Suck.

1. Get the baby warm by swaddling.

ONE SWADDLED BABY

A great instructional drawing on how to swaddle — and it's important — can be found at: moms4mom.com/questions/3217/how-do-you -swaddle-a-baby.

2. Turn him on stomach or side.

3. Very loudly say, "Shhhhh." You must say that louder than the baby is crying and keep right on saying it. If you're in public, you'll be embarrassingly loud. Remember hearing those swooshing noises when you saw the fetus with ultrasound? That's what you're trying to replicate.

4. Swing the hell out of it. You can do this with the baby in your arms or in a sling or car seat.

5. Give him something to suck. Your little finger will do. A pacifier is fine. Some people will be against the use of a pacifier, but if it's fine with your wife, no problem. At least you can take it away, unlike a

thumb. There is only one truth about pacifiers: the position of your wife's sisters and your mother-in-law will be the opposite of yours.

My first daughter used a pacifier that kept getting lost in the night. Eventually she went to bed with four. One for her mouth, one for each hand, and a spare. She spun the ones in her hands between her fingers like majorette batons.

A friend of mine took a pacifier away from her son when he was about three. She just threw it in the trash can one day, frustrated. That night she sat on the couch with her husband after putting the baby down without his pacifier. The two of them were waiting for all hell to break loose. In addition to the pacifier, the son liked to go to sleep cuddling a couple of clean cloth diapers. After about fifteen minutes, my friend heard her son call, "Mommy?" She went in. He was holding a cloth diaper in each hand. He said, "Might as well take these, too."

**!

If all else fails, here's an alternative way to stop the baby from crying — after it's a few months old and able to hold its head up: toss it into the air.

I learned the toss-up trick from Caleb. It has worked for me lots of times. Just be sure to catch the baby on the way down. Actually you don't have to toss her high. Just a few inches — your hands at her armpits. (My theory is that the baby is surprised and forgets what the crying was about.) You might want to first try this alone with the baby in some back room, and then if it works, your wife will probably start doing it while her mother is not around. If your mother-in-law objects, and if you're big enough, toss *her* into the air.

Cultures that treat the baby like it's still in the womb for those first three months have quiet babies in general, say some baby books. After the birth, those mothers may carry the baby in a sling, and Mother and Father sleep with the baby. I'm not for sleeping with the baby, though some paren-tologists and friends are. I like having the baby sleep at the foot of the bed in a bassinet (or cooler) until he's a few months old (then off to his own room or a room with Brother or Sister). That way you can get to the baby quickly in the middle of the night and hand him to your wife if he's hungry and she's breast-feeding, or feed him from a bottle if you're going that route. And by the way, if the baby is sleeping with you in the bed, it's going to be difficult — once your wife is ready again — to get some heavy loving, you know. Plus I worry about how long the sleeping with parents will last. The practice will call for weaning, which could be problematic, especially if your child at age nine or so sees nighttime separation as rejection of some sort, or if he's suddenly drafted into the army.

This "where does baby sleep?" is, as I mentioned, one of those parenting practices debated in parenting literature. The large numbers of variables in play make it hard to reach solid conclusions. A baby sleeping with parents who rarely talk to or cuddle the baby may be less free to experience childhood in full than the baby who sleeps on the lawn but is often held and talked to and listened to, eye to eye.

What about *after* those first three months? Will the crying be less? The chances are very high that it will, and you'll be gaining confidence in holding the baby, throwing him in the air, occasionally dropping him. Those first three months are crazy — you're doing all you can to make the baby happy. That's as it should be.

At about three to maybe as late as five months, you should *not* (barring different instructions from your child's doctor because of an unusual problem, or because of failure to follow my upcoming advice) be getting up in the night, staggering into Baby's room to feed or otherwise care for the baby. The child should be sleeping through the night. *THE*

BABY'S STOMACH NOW HOLDS ENOUGH FOOD AND WATER TO LAST THROUGH THE NIGHT!

Once more: after about three to five months (maybe six?), you should *not* (unless your child's doctor insists) be needing to get up in the night to feed the baby or otherwise care for him — unless you just like to do that sort of thing. Remember, the first three months are when the baby is supposed to be in the womb, and that's why after the first few weeks (of your infatuation and adrenaline) after the baby leaves the womb, you might discover some pure hell for three- to four-hour stretches of baby screaming and crying at all hours of the night.

However. However, it will be, barring an act of God, almost impossible after the first three or four months to break yourself from getting up in the middle of the night over and over to try to *somehow* quiet your crying baby: with mama's breast, food, reading, cuddling, dancing, walking while holding baby, driving her in a car seat until she falls back asleep (I used to search for stretches of road with certain kinds of bumps that seemed to be best for inducing baby sleep — there are some that are two blocks east of the downtown square in Medina, Ohio), making faces at her, singing to her, showing her herself in a handheld mirror, putting on a puppet show for her, or using the 5 S's. In other words, something that worked in the first three months.

Listen. You and your wife will need nighttime rest. Entire, uninterrupted nights of rest. I want to prepare you for what's coming while you're reading this, before you're confronted with sleepless nights going into month six or seven or eight — a time when you should be alert and awake during daylight hours.

Here's a Method for Parental and Baby Sleep—loosely adapted from Richard Ferber's book: *Solve Your Child's Sleep Problems.* The method may have to be applied more than once. By that I mean that the Method for Parental and Baby Sleep will take only three to seven or eight days to implement, but after six months to a year you might need to reimplement.

1. Go through your put-Baby-to-bed routine, place the baby in her crib, pat her, speak to her. LEAVE THE ROOM. Start any kind of timer (on the microwave, for example)—set on ten minutes. (Eight or twelve minutes will work just as well.) DO NOT GO BACK INTO THE BABY'S ROOM BEFORE THE TIMER GOES OFF! (This may be extremely hard to accomplish.)

2. When the timer goes off, go back into the baby's room and say anything you like. Pat the baby on the back or tummy or side, depending on which is up. LEAVE THE ROOM—with the baby still in her crib, crying or not. Remember: *this is after the baby is three or four, maybe five or six, months old. Many doctors say three months.*

3. Go back to your timing device. Set it for twelve minutes (or two minutes beyond the first time). Repeat number 2 above as many times as you have to before Baby falls asleep. Increase the timer two minutes each time. When the baby stops crying, go to bed and to sleep.

On the next night go through this procedure again.

I know—almost impossible. But here's what's happening— the baby is *learning to go to sleep on her own,* learning to take care of herself, whereas previously she thought she couldn't go to sleep without your or her mother's help. She's not crying because she's hurting. She's crying because she's unhappy. If you think something unusual is wrong with the baby, take her to the doctor for a checkup.

If the baby cries in the night, start the method again by waiting for ten minutes before going in.

After the second or third night, your mother or mother-in-law or the vegetarian will verbally blister you for this "inhumane" practice.

Persevere if you can, but you need your wife on board.

This procedure will be one of the most difficult to implement methods for *anything* you will ever do. My educated guess is that at approximately the five- or six-night mark, maybe after three nights, you'll be shocked. *Your baby will sleep through the night.* Ah, bliss. Same the next night. And the next. She's learned to put herself to sleep — she doesn't need the old routines.

In a few months, she may get sick and you will have to attend her throughout several nights, and then when she's well again, you'll find you need to reinstate the Method for Parental Sleep if you wish to clear yourself from the midnight madness that prevents you from being a rested parent in the daytime.

With the second child and later children, you will automatically and with surprising ease implement the Method for Parental and Baby Sleep.

I've thought this through, and my guess is the method above is to ease the parents into solving the problem. If you could stand it and go cold turkey — let Baby cry himself to sleep a few nights in a row — I think the problem might be solved more quickly. But it's hard *not* to go in there and do something. The method above allows for that.

TV

The American Academy of Pediatrics says to keep the baby away from TV before age two. And as I mentioned earlier, after two, especially given a segment of our population's obsession with selling products to children. I can't get it past my brain that it takes a slimy bastard to plead to *small children* to buy his or her product.

. . . .

THREE AND A HALF YEARS OLD

Nathaniel,

Well, buddy, your new little sister is home from the hospital, and you like to baby talk to her and hug her and sit on the bed and hold her. She's just beginning to take in her world, and on the night of the day she came you announced *that there was no longer room for you in this family* and that you couldn't live here anymore with Mama and Papadaddy, and you were crying and your big sister was talking to you and then I was talking to you. You were under the dining room table with no clothes on. And after a brief talk, you crawled out, stood, and said, "I was just teasing." But of course you weren't and that night you and I talked and I told you how important you were to all of us, and you stood in the bed after we read our story and hugged me with a long hug. The day before you had put pages from your coloring book, with a little bit of color on each page, in the hall, in your room, in our room, in the kitchen, and in the sunroom. And a day after your little sister came home from the hospital, you peed in the trash can, and then a few nights later, you spread baby powder all over the guest bedroom, a whole container of it, on furniture, on the walls, and other furniture, and finally, on the rug in a pile.

Every night we play Delbert McClinton's *Never Been Rocked Enough* CD and you dance and dance and dance to "Every Time I Roll the Dice," and just today I tested you to see if you could keep different rhythms and you could! You're bunches of fun and you helped me blow leaves the other day and also put together a bookcase kind of piece for the back porch.

I love you,
Papadaddy

*C.O.D.

One of the experiences I had growing up in rural North Carolina in the late 1940s and '50s (I was born in 1944) was that of living in a community — "community" meaning something like this: the one or two hundred people who lived there knew a lot about each other. That time and place and local culture colors how I think about my children now. The chance that you—an older dad—experienced something like this is greater than for young dads. It perhaps influences our parenting in ways I can't fathom. The children (white) all went to the same elementary and high school, and most of us went to the same church. This was before integration in my region, and it was as if my people were from a different country than rural black people nearby. But as it turns out, I share much with them in terms of food, religion, time outdoors experiencing the drama of fishing, hunting, baseball, and other games UNsupervised by adults.

It turns out that in my present community many of us know each other as parents, and consequently I know the parents of my children's friends. Because of this, I'm more comfortable about what my children are doing when they are visiting friends' homes than when I lived in another place twenty years ago and my first daughter spent time in homes of people I didn't know. Back then we lived more or less alone in the woods, away from a "community," and I never thought much about what I'm writing about right now.

About all I can do here is point out the comfort that can come from knowing the parents of your children's friends. I cherish my present setup, and I suggest that you try to get to know the parents of your children's friends. I think you'd want to think twice about allowing your children to spend the night with children whose parents hold fundamentally different values from yours, or at least be able to discuss those differences with your child.

SAFE SLEEP

Once you get the baby home, you will read instructions about safe practices for how (in what position on a mattress) your baby should sleep. These instructions are from your doctor's office. This document will say that if the baby sleeps on her back then she will die from inhaling vomit, and that if she sleeps on her stomach she will die of SIDS (sudden infant death syndrome), and that if she sleeps on her left or right side her heart will stop because of arrhythmia. There will be a prescription for a $535 device that you can order from a man in Detroit. The device will look like a long-legged tripod and will have several straps from which you can suspend your child by the chin and knees for safe sleeping.

I do not doubt the statistics on SIDS; however, my emphasis as a father of newborns was in keeping stuffed toys and pillows out of the bassinet. Check each night. Once the baby can lift her head, chances of SIDS will be greatly reduced—and that will happen within a few months.

MAMA CRYING

Postpartum depression for Mom may be significant.

Bathe the baby, change diapers, hold her, and take her to the store so Mama can miss her. Be on call for your mate. Be ready for stress.

NEIGHBORS WHO VISIT

An older woman neighbor you've never met will come by for a visit on the second day you are home.

She will have shingles.

She will explain that shingles is not contagious, but that her grandson had some skin disease so bad he had to be bathed in Vaseline and wrapped in pajamas soaked in vinegar, and that whatever you do, don't touch the umbilical cord stub, because it will get infected—and that it needs to be covered in a mix of Vaseline and iodine—and she'll say that if the child gets a fever over 104.5 he will never be right again. And that a fever can shoot up in the middle of the night in no time at all. She will leave a gift—a small picture frame with plastic animals glued to it, several of which have fallen off.

When she's out of sight, you'll remember that she warned you about "red spots." "They can get real infected if you don't watch out," she will have said. You will casually go in to check your sleeping baby and find nine to fourteen red spots.

POOP, PEE, WIPES, AND DIAPERS

"There are three main systems: the bowl siphon, the flush mechanism and the refill..."

CLeaRLY ·ExPlaining HoW a ToILet Functions is the Most ImpoRtant steP IN SuCcessFul PotTY TRaining.

Someone will have given you several boxes of "wipes." Each wipe is like a thick, damp Kleenex. They make tasks like cleaning the baby relatively quick and easy. You will have seen them at the hospital. Consider buying them in bulk and placing them into the smaller plastic boxes you get from your grocery store or pharmacy.

The choice in diapers can be overwhelming. Inserts, flips, reusables, disposables, greens, quicks, slows, safes, tights, looses, slim fit, relaxed fit, tapered, shrink to fit, boot cut, and flares. Your wife will probably, on advice of friends, make all necessary decisions. For a quick overview, three options follow:

1. *Disposable diapers.* If the vegetarian will be coming around, think twice about this option. And listen, if you do use this option, don't get one of those plastic cans, sort of like a covered trash can, for disposable diapers. It has a revolving switchback device up top that dumps dirty diapers down into a tall plastic garbage bag while, quote, not releasing a bad smell, end quote. Man, that thing is a big pain in the ass. It will start stinking because of stray feces that get hung in these cracks in the revolving top, which gets stuck all the time, and you will become very frustrated out in the backyard *pressure washing* the thing.

   Here's what to do with disposable diapers (if you decide not to use the cloth ones — which are far less problem than you might think): ball up the pee diapers and throw them in any trash can in the house. Put a stinky diaper in a plastic (biodegradable) grocery bag, tie the opening shut, place it outside the door, and next time you go to the outside garbage can, take it along for discarding. If you're picky, do the pee diaper the same way.

2. *A diaper service.* You just put dirty cloth diapers in a laundry bag; the truck picks them up and leaves clean diapers. You'll want to of course shake poop off as necessary — in the commode. (You can kind of swish it around in there without getting your hand

in. Then flush. You can also keep a spatula in the
commode brush holder.)

3. *Cloth diapers,* without the service. Rinse poop off as
   necessary, put them in your dirty clothes hamper,
   wash and dry them and use them again. Sprinkle
   baking soda in the hamper once in a while. This
   choice is less trouble than you might think. For
   details about this and other diaper questions, check
   the website diaperpin.com. NOTE: baking soda paste
   (made with a little water and baking soda) is great for
   deodorant and/or toothpaste—I'm talking about for
   you, not the baby necessarily. The baby shouldn't
   need deodorant for a while. I remember spending the
   night with a new friend when I was thirteen and his
   mother asked me if I'd started using deodorant and I
   said no, and she said it was time. They'd moved in
   from out of town—first friend whose parents had
   gone to college. In some ways it's been downhill since.

TWO YEARS OLD

Catherine,

We just got home and the babysitter said she was
changing your diaper and you said, "My mama and
daddy think I still have to have a diaper."

Love,

Daddy

• • •

You can buy a tiny commode seat that sits on top of a regular one, kind of like some older people use. But I wouldn't do that. If you need to have one of those, then you're training too early, in my view. Of course, you can read articles about babies being trained to use the toilet before they can lift their heads. I suggest that those parents may spend an inordinate amount of time in training. (So, okay, we're getting into your business here — you might want to skip ahead, but this is part of the job.) And don't use the little commode with the recording of a flush; it has a plastic insert bowl and it's so little that a small boy trying to piss in it can't hit it, so you'll have to clean up the floor every time it's used, and then poop will need to be dumped out, followed by clean up.

By the time my youngest child came along, we'd just prop her on the edge of the commode seat for potty training.

For the potty training part — every mama friend of your wife's will have a method. It's a matter of talking to the child, predicting when he needs to go to the bathroom, taking him, and then preparing for accidents.

Just be sure you *never ever* punish a child at *any* age for a pee or poop accident.

Oh, that reminds me — if you carry your glasses or cell phone or pens in your shirt pocket, you'll start losing them in the commode when you bend over to wipe your child who's not yet large enough to cover the commode opening.

> ****!**
>
> ***Don't keep pens and glasses in your
> shirt pocket anymore.***

While we're on this topic: I once took my very small son into the men's room at a restaurant. He got in a stall, locked it, sat on the commode, and pooped. He'd never wiped himself. He noticed that I was locked out of the stall. He said, "Hey, how're we going to handle this?"

> ****!**
>
> ***If your child is asking very intelligent and well-
> thought-out questions that are beyond you, it
> might be time to teach him to wipe himself.***

I told him to stand and unlock the door. He did and we finished. Back out in the restaurant, he said to everyone at the table, "I could have been in there for days and days."

BATHS

For a very small baby, warm water, baby soap, a kitchen sink, and a soft washrag and drying towel are all you need. Get into the creases where fungus can thrive, and keep the baby's head out of the water. Of course you don't plop the baby down in a sink full of cold water. You make the water warm, hold him at the edge of the sink, and splash water on his feet. Then get him down in the water, holding him securely with one hand, bathing with the other. He might jerk loose, go under, and come back up screaming. Just try not to drop him on the kitchen floor. Have some fun, and at about six weeks, during a bath, or while you're holding him, or when he's looking up just after a nap, he's going to smile at you for the first time. You'll be so blown away that you'll need to write that down somewhere. A journal (paper or digital) is a good place to keep notes and letters to your child. The day of the first bath or the first smile might be the day you start it. Can you imagine reading a note to you from your father about the first bath he gave you? (Not interested? I'll try to calm down a little.)

Bathing the baby is a job the mother may not want you to have, but on the other hand, you walking in and saying "I think I'll bathe the baby" could make her day, week, month, year.

If you wonder about whether you should give your baby a bath on a particular night and you are very tired, remember that you're only about twenty-four short hours away from tomorrow night. Once your baby starts crawling and then walking, dirt will of course be more apparent on knees and feet. Sometimes when you're supposed to give a two-year-old a bath and you can't wait twenty-four hours, wipe off her hands and the bottoms of her feet with a wipe and run a wet washrag through her hair and wipe dirt rings from around her neck and wipe her butt with another wipe. Dampen a towel, place it over her shoulder, and send her in to Mama to say, "Aw quean, Mommy."

DAY DUTIES

If your wife does most of the work around the house, consider picking up some, or most, or all objects that are out of place in the baby's room (and/or other rooms) and putting them in their proper place. Once a day might work. Take up slack in other ways. If you're the one who stays home in the daytime, be sure you sit down and talk with your wife about how she might best help when she comes home in the afternoon. Whatever the arrangement, I suggest that you talk, talk, talk.

If you have each staked out a position in an ongoing disagreement and deep down you hear a voice saying, "You could give up your position and the world wouldn't end," then consider giving it up. If the going gets rough, it may be helpful for each of you to say what you fear. That can cut through anger, sometimes.

NIGHT-FEEDING DUTIES

If your wife is breast-feeding, you should share night-feeding duties with her. That means when the baby starts crying just as you're falling to sleep, you pick the baby up from the cooler at the foot of the bed and bring him to your wife's side. Some book will have instructed you to always keep track of which breast she used *last* by noting L for left and R for right in a small notebook. But the best way is to sort of juggle both breasts to see which one is heavier. This will normally wake her up. But if she won't wake up, whisper that you want to make love, and she will try to escape, thus waking up. Unbutton her pajamas and prepare the baby for the appropriate breast. The hungry baby's head will bob and jerk around while he looks cross-eyed for anything that resembles a nipple. You should keep him away from the bedside radio because he will suck the knobs off it.

The baby will bite your wife's nipples for the first few weeks of breast-feeding, making her scream. The baby's gums are like brass knuckles. But your wife loves the baby and will forget all this. When the baby finishes nursing, take the baby from your wife, tell her to go back to sleep, and you change the baby's diaper. If you've been doing your job, you'll be handling the baby as you saw the nurses at the hospital handling her, swaddling, picking up, holding, carrying.

If you and your wife are bottle-feeding the baby, then somebody will have to feed the baby every two or three hours around the clock at first, and in a few months the nighttime feeding will be down to twice a night and then once a night. If it's okay with your wife, there's no reason you shouldn't be feeding the baby in the night. I fed my first child, Catherine (from when she was a couple of months old to five months), at about three every morning when she woke up and cried. It was a very special time. She'd look at me, I'd look at her, and she'd drink from the bottle until she was full and drifting off to sleep. I looked forward to that time. I felt both pleased and a little sad when she started sleeping through the night.

Your wife will be involved with breast matters big-time if she's breast-feeding. Sometimes her breasts will oversupply and they'll need relief. Did your mother breast-feed? Yes? Well? It's not a bad taste at all, and certainly the two of you will have talked about resuming sex — how, when, how often, and all that — and so...I mean, why not? What kind of man are you?

You may be wondering about how long to wait for sex after the baby comes.

Two weeks to a year.

Settling In

SPOILING, SCHEDULING, CHARTING

Please get very clear on this: you can't spoil a child who is under three or four months old. Your job when he is that young is to give him food and drink and comfort whenever you can—as you move him toward firm but changeable schedules for eating and napping. I always made charts with times that seemed to be working for sleeping. Even though the child is very young, you can move him toward a schedule—starting as soon as a schedule begins developing.

UP- at about 6:30

NAP- 9:30 - 11:30

LUNCH

NAP - 2:30 - 4:30

BeDTiMe - 6:30

After a year or so, the morning nap or afternoon nap will stop working and then the other nap will be needed up to age five or so. But don't count on anybody else's dictation of a schedule. Normally, no two children will need the same sleep schedule. But babies need a lot of rest and sleep, and you should help see that yours get it.

Oddly enough, early on, more napping probably means better sleeping at night. A mother I know was keeping her kid up in the day so he would sleep at night, and she was unable to understand why the child didn't sleep at night. It was because he was too tired to sleep, too wired from lack of rest.

After three or four months or so, we'll worry about spoiling. Because at some point between six months and a year the baby may start running the household, and you don't want to live in a house run by a baby, though some experts will in so many ways tell you that that is the path to glory. In part four of this book we'll get more into behavior management and such—a crucial area for your, and the baby's, sanity.

TALKING TOYS: SATAN IS REAL AND THESE ARE AMONG HIS GIFTS

Children usually like to play with old pots and pans—and blocks of wood, and paper, crayons, and pencils. But watch out for bungee cords. One may be stretched from just behind the driver's seat in the car, turned loose, and rip your ear off. This starts when your child is old enough to hold his head up and uncross his eyes.

Far worse than bungee cords, in general, is one of Satan's gifts to Earth: *talking toys*. Some sing. Let's say it's singing "Jingle Bells"; it will not sing the whole song, just the chorus. Three times on each button push.

For a while after Nathaniel (my older son) was born, I'd turn out the lights at night in the playroom and one of his toys would screech: "Good night!" And I do mean *screech*.

I couldn't find it because it would only talk in the dark. One night I removed all the toys from Nathaniel's big toy box (if there's more than one toy box per child, there may be too many toys in your house) and put them on a table and cut the light out, and none of them would say a word. Then back in the toy box it started in talking again a few nights later. *"Good night!"*

After a week or so, I caught it—a little plastic man. I tied it up, put it under the back tire of our car, and backed over it. The sound—the pop and scattering of it on the concrete driveway—was most satisfying.

One suggestion is to buy only used toys. If we started recycling them as we do other plastic things, the world would be a better place. But this probably won't happen. Toys are reproducing far faster than humans, I'm guessing.

Just when we got our last child out of diapers, she was given a baby doll that could eat, talk, pee, and poop. (If you're an expectant dad and think I'm spending too much time on pee and poop, you won't in a year.)

Egg cartons make nice houses. Plastic straws are great toys, and a great investment is to buy about three hundred of those clear plastic pint cups that are used for outdoor beer parties. They come in several bright colors and can be arranged into castles, houses, and bridges, and kicked down. And they can be stacked conveniently inside each other for storage.

SLEEP PROBLEMS — YOURS

After Baby comes, you'll probably have problems sleeping at first, because for the first three or four months, as I've said, you let Baby rule the roost and he'll be crying in the middle of the night and you and your wife will comfort him however you can. This is that *fourth* trimester, remember, when he's supposed to be in the womb, as some of our evolutionists tell us.

You and your wife, by the way, because of sleep deprivation and fatigue, will learn new things about each other. If you're working to gain confidence as a father, and you believe in your role and she in hers, then this learning can make you closer to your wife. For the first time in your lives together you may be feeling a unifying purpose stronger than you've ever felt.

Or, you may both be going bonkers and having disagreements — and this will not be abnormal if not in the extreme. During this time you may wonder at the courage and stamina of only one parent (usually a woman) doing the job of raising a kid alone.

PLAYING WITH BABY

After the first few months (or before), act silly. Put odd things on your head. Talk goofy and make funny faces. Slobber. Pretend you are a dog, a turkey, a computer scientist. Get down on the floor with your children as often as you can; talk to them and listen to them. If your father was the silent type, this behavior may not come naturally.

If you're very tired when your child requests playtime on the floor, then you can get down there, doze off, and let him play on you.

. . . .

FIFTEEN MONTHS

Ridley,

You accidentally fell from a high front porch table day before yesterday, face-first onto the deck, and you ended up with scratches and a fat lip but healed quickly. You do tongue tricks when I show you how, and you crack up at all sorts of antics. You're lovable and have fun with just about anything.

Love,

Papadaddy

. . . .

*C.O.D.

I once taught a student who had had seventy-five siblings—seventy-three were foster siblings. She wrote about it, and she seemed to be a healthy, happy individual. I don't think I could be an adult with so many little people in the house over the years, but some people can, and one of the difficulties in composing a book like this is to take into account the different dispositions of parents. But if you are an older dad, then we probably have one thing in common: we think about parenting with a tiny fear that our kids might have to mature without us.

And none of us can help but think about how many children we want. If you're thinking about having a third child, or a second, even, you should perhaps go ahead and take the plunge if you can afford it. Consider the following. One: when you're in a wheelchair and one child is pushing, the second can open doors. The addition of a third will, if you can afford another child, not make a lot of practical difference. You just put out an additional plate, recycle toys, and eat a lot of leftovers. It can be a little more like a fun group outing when you go somewhere, rather than a small family outing.

The drawback is that with three there may be more vying for your attention when the family is all together — a little more competition than if you have one or two. You'll be astonished when you get just one child off alone at a meal or at a movie or on a short trip. Wonderful peace and quiet and conversation come about. He or she has your undivided attention and becomes a different human being while away from siblings — no teasing the other children (smaller ones will tease older ones as much as it goes the other way), no hitting, getting hit, pinching, spitting, calling names.

(continued)

No two siblings interact the same way, but all, it seems, say they hate each other at times. One of my cousins murdered his brother. Not Caleb.

Another point about having the second or third. The second two are less trouble while in the womb. Not "trouble," but "distraction," or attention getting. An illustration: with the first of my last three in the womb, I'd sing songs to him most every day and put my ear to Kristina's stomach to listen in on the squirshing around in there. (I listened the same way to my first daughter thirty years ago.) I'd write him a letter every few days. Then with the second of my last three—twenty-three months after the first—the attention and preparations were less, and then with the third it was significantly less. I even feel guilty about the sparseness of letters I wrote to Truma, my youngest, before she was born, and I probably sang to her in the womb only a few times. But now at age six, and the youngest, she has my attention in part because she's the youngest.

And of course with four, you have an opportunity to marvel at their different temperaments. If our dog throws up, one child (commas—like the last one—can be important) may well also throw up while another gathers the vomit in a dustpan and feeds it back to the dog (who'll eat it if we're lucky).

READING TO BABY

You can't start reading to the baby too early, even though she won't know what you're doing at first. But she will see a book and see pages and see words. And once she understands what you're doing, the best way to handle some of those sentimental children's stories is to thumb through the book and say "bird" and point to one. "Dog" and so forth. Before long you can say the word and the child will point. And that will be big. Ask the child where the cow is, where the moon is and all that. Wait until the children are older to worry about reading the text. And then don't read sentimental fluff to them. Read them the original Brothers Grimm. a) That will hold their attention, and b) they damn sure won't get up and wander around the house after lights out.

Also, please read any dialect stories in their original (and beautiful) dialects, not in the "Standard English" texts. Out in the world and in written stories, both standard *and* nonstandard dialects can be powerful and beautiful. Some of us who were overtaught about "correct English" miss out on what spoken dialects have to offer in spice, color, and meaning. Most linguists know that there are no "incorrect" usages, that specific words and usages and grammars often have more or less power depending on the context and situation in which they are used.

A good idea is to find a neighbor child who's a few years older than yours (and perhaps whose mother or father is a teacher of some sort). Ask the parents if you can buy their old books, and they'll probably start giving them to you. (This could also work with clothes.)

Truma,

You went through a rough spell about a week ago, not wanting to go to sleep. You'd say, "Fan on," and then when I turned it on, you'd say, "Fan off," and this went on for several nights until I said it'd have to be one way or the other, and then you'd cry in distress until somebody came in and talked. We figured out that talking to you carefully and slowly right before putting you down made a difference. And you've been doing great since. At night we talk over what happened during the day. The ritual is this. We go to your room with about a third of a bottle of milk — in a plastic sippy cup. You drink while we read the first of three books; then we read another. You'll supply words, especially with the Spot books, and then we march into the bathroom, singing, "Brusha Brusha Brusha, new Ipana toothpaste. Brusha, Brusha, Brusha, Ipana for your TEEEETH." You join me on the some of the words, especially "TEEEETH," and then you let me brush your teeth, and then you brush, and then we have fun flossing with these little throwaway floss things; we grunt in unison, sort of saying "Flossa Flossa Flossa." After brushing we play basketball by throwing our little floss sticks into the trash can.

I love you,
Papadaddy

CURSING IN FRONT OF BABY

After the baby starts mimicking you, you will curse one day and the baby will say the same words. You must be prepared for this. Let's say you cut your finger — and then say words I can't print because of the sensibilities of older relatives.

The baby hears you and repeats the curse words.

Be prepared. Say, "No, no. Sheet got down. Daddy's playing a game. Daddy is a sheet and he's going to get down on the floor." And you spread your arms, get down on the floor and roll over, and tell the baby to do the same thing. In the meantime, you're dripping blood on the carpet. Then you repeat, "Sheet got down" and roll over once more.

You will need to think ahead, come up with stories that fit all your curse words or maybe confine your cursing to words that fit the stories. Maybe buy a rubber duck.

The baby will spread his arms and get down on the floor and say, "Sheet got down."

See, that's all there is to it.

Then your mother-in-law walks in and the baby repeats the curse words and then says "Daddy say" and repeats them again.

CHORES
(consider calling them "Activities")

Some could be: feed the dog, feed the fish, feed the chickens, water the lawn, sweep, trash out, dusting, do some laundry work, pick up shoes, help stack wood, bring in wood. Help empty dishwasher. Fold clothes, place pillows where they belong. Make up bed. Pick up toys. A regular schedule with a chart that keeps tabs is a good idea.

Telling children what they should do while not requiring compliance on a systematic basis can create frustrating situations. But talking to them about why they need to do chores will help things move along. And because of the time consumed in teaching these activities, it may be tempting for you to give up trying, so a good idea is to start very small, say, with one chore, and build from there...so that by the time they are eighteen they have two chores.

STUFF YOUR CHILDREN WILL SAY
TO EACH OTHER AND TO YOU
(and what to say back, sometimes)

"Daddy, where's my bicycle helmet? I got something I want to try off the deck."

"Don't do it."

———

"When you go to college, are parrots allowed on campus?"
"I guess. Why would you want a parrot on campus?"
"Everybody has a parrot."
"*You* don't."
"*You're* my parent."
"Oh, yes."

———

This from my six-year-old when I'm trying to get him to do his homework and he's interested in playing on the floor with me. When I say, "Do your homework," he says, "Now, tell me, which do you think is more important, homework or family?"

———

Kristina and I explain to our six-year-old daughter that a child who is different from us in some ways is coming to visit. The child is unable to do some of the things we're used to doing with ease. We search for the right words. We stress that the child is no less precious and worthy because she is different.

The child and mother enter our house.

My daughter says loudly to the child: "You don't look so different."

———

After the first day of kindergarten, be prepared for your child to say, at the dinner table, as ours did: "Anybody in this family who's stuck your finger in your butt, raise your hand."

For a second you will wonder what to do, but you should be honest with your children.

———

Our new housecleaner comes into our living room. Our three-year-old says: "We had another housecleaner. She's probably dead."

———

In a bathroom at a gas station one day, your six-year-old son will point to the prophylactic machine and say, "Can I have one of those?"

"No."

You might add, "Not yet."

———

Once, just after I'd complimented Catherine for putting on her seat belt without being asked (she was probably three years old), I asked her why she wore a seat belt. She said, "To keep from bumping my head." I said, "Good answer." She said, "Well, it was a good question."

———

Once, after Mama kissed Ridley (then aged five) good night, he said, "Mama, when you kiss me good night and I wipe off your kiss, I put it on my heart."

———

If your child is two and the children's vitamin container says she's allowed only a half of a vitamin and the vitamins are in the shape of little animals, and your child howls "Noooooo" and starts bawling when you cut a little vitamin kitty in half, then you probably should not look at the other half and say, *"Bad* kitty."

———

We were at a friend's house eating dinner and the wind was gusting, bending trees. Nathaniel (aged three) looked at the trees and said, "Look, the trees are laughing." And we said, "At what?" and he said, "At us eating dinner." About twenty-five years before, watching leaves falling from trees, Catherine said, "The trees are crying."

———

We were in a sports equipment store to buy soccer shoes for Ridley. The saleswoman took us to the shoe wall and said, "Why don't you pick a shoe you'd like?" Ridley (aged five) looked for a minute and then said to her, "Excuse me, ma'am, but which one would you pick if you were choosing?"

———

My older daughter—as a child—once asked if Mr. Rogers had a "thing." Susan, her mother, said, "That's a good question."

———

We're riding in the car and Truma, the youngest, says, "Can we have some chewing gum?" Kristina says, "I don't have any chewing gum." Ridley says, "If you *did,* could we have some?"

At some point you will be gathered with your boys at the commode and you'll each be urinating and you'll spit your chewing gum into the commode. One of the boys will bend over to do the same and you'll pee on his head and he'll look up at you with a funny look and ask, "Did you pee on my head?"

You should be honest with your children.

WHAT YOU DO AND SAY THAT THEY'LL REMEMBER

Your important pronouncements will most likely be forgotten, and apparently insignificant words remembered.

After somebody stole a sock full of silver dollars from my room when I was about sixteen, I was sitting on our front porch with my mother. We had just searched the house high and low. I was angry. I said, "I don't know who took that money, but he's a damn son of a bitch." My mother, stunned, said, "Son, I didn't even know you *thought* words like that." Her words have stayed with me. I can't begin to imagine all her moral guidance throughout my early life — the directions for living that I don't remember. I do remember the Billy Graham tracts she sent me while I was in the Air Force, but not much about what they said. What was never discarded was the unspoken message from my mother: "I care about you, who you become."

I have friends who are brothers. While they remember a good bit their father said to them, one brother told me he *clearly* remembers a sentence spoken often in their childhood and adolescence by their banjo-picking, storytelling father — even though the contexts now escape him: "Son, have you lost your damn mind?"

I remember sitting on the couch beside my father when I was about seven. He needed a shave, and I put my cheek to his cheek to feel his beard. I happened to look through the dining room window and saw some telephone poles and wires. I thought to myself, I'll never forget this, and I never have.

I remember Uncle Bob teaching me, when I was eight, to cast an open-faced spinning reel. A weight was tied to the end of the line. We were in his backyard. He'd just shown me the placement of the thumb, explained the mechanics of a backlash. I cast the weight, and as the line spun out, I watched a terrible backlash bunch up at the reel. I wondered what Uncle Bob would say. What he said was "You sure —ed that up." I had no idea what that strange word meant, but it seemed significant. I've never forgotten the moment, in part because my blood told me that a significant word had been spoken.

Kristina remembers playing in a backyard with other children when she was six. She was shirtless. An uncle said, "Put on a shirt, girl."

I guess it's conceivable that if we say something too many times to our children, like "Sit up straight," a little barrier is set up that begins blocking that particular message. Eventually, the child forgets forever what you say over and over. Thus, my children will never remember my saying, "Where are your SHOES?"

Here's a warning, though. Don't ever say to a child, "Are you getting a little chubby?" Many of you reading this have more sense than I do. And my thirty-year-old daughter, Catherine, has, reasonably, never forgotten my saying that to her. Her college thesis was about adolescent girls' body images.

Another of my uncles said these things to me:

"Did you check the air in the tires? You never check the air in the tires, do you?"

"If you keep throwing curveballs, you'll ruin your arm."

One day when I was fourteen, I walked into the general store near home. This uncle and several older men were sitting around. One of the men said, "That boy's about to be a man, ain't he?" and my uncle said, "Not that one."

This uncle lived off and on with my mother, father, and me while I was growing up — usually for six months at a time (he'd spend the next six months with another of his sisters) — and surely we talked some, though not much, and perhaps he once said something encouraging to me, but if so, I don't remember what it was. And when he was very intoxicated, he called me by another nephew's name.

GAMES AND BEDTIME STORIES FOR AGES 2–5

(note: some games are good for any age)

SKY TELEVISION: Place a blanket or sleeping bags on the lawn (or on the roof of your house), and lie on your back with the rest of the family. Watch the sky as if you're watching TV, and talk to one another about what you are seeing. We once saw a hawk fly by carrying a snake. Of course we see clouds shaped like dogs, bulls, birds, dolphins, and faces. On clear nights we see satellites moving across the sky.

HERE, LITTLE PIGGY: Let's say your daughter doesn't like scrambled eggs, but you want her to eat them. Well, sit next to her at the breakfast table; get some egg from her plate onto a fork, and while looking back over your shoulder, move the fork to a position a foot or so from her mouth. Call out, "Come here, Little Piggy [you are pretending a little piggy has just entered the room while you continue to hold the fork near her mouth]. I've got some egg for you to eat, Little Piggy. Come on now. There you are. Right over here, Little Piggy." On the first try at this game you may need to whisper to your child, "Eat the egg before Little Piggy does!" Then you look back at the piggy and call to him again. When the piggy gets there and you lower the now-empty fork, you say, "Here you go, Little Piggy...oh, my *goodness!* What in the world happened to your *egg?!*"

Your daughter will *not* say, "Let's play something else." She'll say, "Do it again." And she'll eat the hell out of that egg.

PRETEND TO READ: After you read a story to a child, hand her the book and ask her to read (or tell) the story back to you as she turns the pages. You may be surprised at what happens. You're giving her a sudden great burst of power.

RIDE A LITTLE HORSEY DOWN TO TOWN (OLDIE BUT GOODIE): You're seated, child on knees, and while bouncing the child, you say, "Ride a little horsey down to town. Better watch out or you might fall..." Here you spread your legs and let the child fall toward the floor — as you hold her — while you say "Down."

RUN LIKE A RABBIT: If you can play guitar, make up a little song that uses a couple of chords. You simply sing these words. "Hop like a rabbit, hop like a rabbit, oh hop, hop, hop like a rabbit, hop." If you don't play music, then say the words while you stomp your foot and/or clap your hands. The child hops around the room or from room to room like a rabbit. And after a few times of that, change the song to "Swim like a fish, swim like a fish, oh swim, swim, swim like a fish, swim." The child gets on the floor and swims like a fish. Elephant, dolphin, cat, cougar, old person, etc. If you don't think you can do this, reconsider having a child. (If the mood is right, this is also a great song for adults.)

FLASHLIGHT ON CEILING STORY: After the child is in bed, turn out the lights and shine a flashlight onto the ceiling. There will be a circle of light enclosed by darkness, and then you can start practically any scary story. "Once upon a time, Johnny and Mary were way down in a well." (You may need to say "hole" if an open well is not part of your child's experience — though this would be a good excuse for a field trip to an open well. Surely you can find a farm with one.) "When they looked up toward the sky, they saw light. All of a sudden a big monster looked down into the well." (Here you place the tip of a finger onto the rim of the flashlight and move the tip a little bit while the monster speaks.) "'Who is that down there in my well?' said the monster. Then he said, 'Come here, monster friend, and look down into my well where somebody is hiding!'" The monster friend comes [another finger tip over the edge of the flashlight rim], and the monsters have a conversation, deciding to leave the children alone this time, and then a big friendly bear comes and throws a rope down and they climb out. (You are allowed to change the story plot.)

If you play this right, then the small children will never suspect that the monster and the bear are your fingertip shadows. Of course, the narrative and characters can all change over time. If an older child seems to be checking out your fingertips during the game, you can pull that child aside, ask him to keep the secret, and then let him make up and tell flashlight stories to a younger child. Consider staying in the room if the smaller child is skittish.

PIN DOWN THE ARM, LEG, UPPER BODY GAME: Sit on the floor with your arms extended straight ahead. Ask your child (children) to push you to the floor. The key is no hitting, and after a struggle the kid always wins. There are all sorts of modifications, of course, depending on how much time you have and how big the kids are. For example, you could just get down on your hands and knees, and their job would be to flatten you out (again without hitting). And watch out — it's not far from "I wonder if that lamp would hurt Daddy if it caught him upside the head?" to "Was she *always* dead?" Don't be afraid to let them make up the rules. And if they're happy with apparently strange setups ("Daddy, you close your eyes and then crawl around the floor trying to find us"), go with those requests as long as you're able. Allowing children to make up rules is part of the fun and adventure.

STRANGE MONOPOLY: It's not unusual for a father to get upset that a game is not going according to his rules—to the way he's always played it. (This has happened to me.) Relax. In Monopoly, why not just let the kids roll the dice and move the tokens. Or, if they go over six places they get a dollar, twelve places gets them two dollars, and for a double they have to put in a dollar. Something simple like that.

MONSTER GAME: You sit in the middle of the floor with several children. When a child hisses, you, the Monster, have three seconds before going to sleep for five seconds. During this time they can touch you, but when you wake up you can grab and tickle them until they hiss again. Many games with small children do not need scores, winners, losers. The journey is the destination.

"FINISH THE SENTENCE" STORIES: You start a bedtime story about anything—all you need is the start. "A little girl was walking down the road when she saw a..." You point to a child to finish the sentence. Let's say the child says, "Dog." You then begin a next sentence. "The little girl said to the dog..." You point to another child. That child might take over, or if the game is difficult for the child, you can say several new sentences in a row.

The story then continues for as long as you like.

I SPY: A parent asks a child to leave the room and then places a thimble, or a cork, etc., in plain sight. Come to think of it, thimbles may not be available to you. Maybe a pencil or a crayon or a button. (For the 2200 AD readers, three objects that, like the hardback book, were threatened by a "replacement.") Ask the child to come back in and find the object. The child then hides the object for the parent to find.

SURPRISE TRICKS ON MOM: If Mom normally goes in to wake up the kids (as happens at our house), you tell them the night before that you'll be in early to dress them and when Mom comes in and turns back the cover, they'll be already dressed! Or when you are or Mom is about to set the table, the children suddenly take over. Or if Mom is sitting by the fire reading, then gather the kids together for a short secret meeting after which they surprise Mom by walking into where she is, silently, and sitting and reading (or pretending to read) a book for ten minutes.

TICKLE STORIES: The children lie on their backs in bed at bedtime (or anytime). You stand or sit next to them. The story may go something like this. "Once upon a time, there were two buzzards. One was named Buzzy, and the other was named Beaky. They sat on top of a hill, talking." Here you put each hand, shaped somewhat like a buzzard, on your head (don't worry if they look a little like rhinos) as the buzzards talk to each other. "Buzzy says, 'I'm hungry.'" Move one hand as if it were talking. "Beaky says, 'I'm hungry too. Do I see two dead possums down there in the road?' 'Why, I believe you do,' says Buzzy. 'Let's go down for a look.'"

Here you start flapping your hands, and the buzzards go flying down for a look. They swoop awfully close to the children and then light back upon the hill again. "'Let's go down for a little nibble to see what they taste like,' says Buzzy. 'Okay,' says Beaky."

The buzzards fly over the kids and swoop in for a little tickle or two and then go back up on the hill. The buzzards then decide to go back for a meal—a good tickle. And then they can settle down on your head (or shoulders) for a night's sleep, talking all the time.

Rather than buzzards, you can use dolphins or sharks in the water, sitting on a reef and talking and deciding to go down and take a nibble of an oyster. Or whatever.

KING OF THE MOUNTAIN GAME: You sit on the couch and keep the kids off. When a child manages to stay on the couch for three seconds, she is the king. You can also play Queen of the Mountain, of course. And also Middle Class Person of the Mountain.

"IF" CONVERSATION GAMES: At the dinner table, ask this question: "If you could be any kind of animal, what would you be and why?" You can expand to color, tool, fish, toy, vehicle, fruit, bird, piece of furniture, or something like "If you were a clock, what time would you be and why?" If more than one child is at the table, this is a good place for each of them to begin to learn respect for the person talking—no interruption while each child talks in turn. These "if" questions can lead to great discussions that touch on all kinds of subjects, especially when you get into the "why?" part. Your always insisting on no interruptions may help establish a family norm. (Fatherhood tasks in real life are usually harder than they sound in a book like this one.)

HIT THE ROAD JACK: Download a recording of Ray Charles singing "Hit the Road Jack." You and a child pretend one of you is the woman and one is the man in the song. Lip-synch the words while acting out the parts. You and the child can switch parts occasionally. Jack should have a small suitcase in hand — or be packing it when the song opens. Jack pleads; the woman scorns him (hands on hips) before he reluctantly takes to the road at the end of the song. You and your child can search for other songs to pantomime, but this one works beautifully because two characters participate. Another good one would be "Baby, It's Cold Outside."

David Grisman and Jerry Garcia have a wonderful album called *Not for Kids Only,* and it can be used for all sorts of pantomime and dancing.

. . . .

ONE MONTH OLD

Catherine,

Tuesday night I saw you laugh for the first time. You'd just had your bottle and were looking over my shoulder at a windowsill. Suddenly a big grin came over your face and you sucked in air, then laughed for about four breaths.

You are happiest after eating. You are very attentive at those times.

I love you,

Daddy

. . . .

NUMBER GAMES: If you walk the dog, take along a child and say, "I'll bet we see another person before you count to forty-one." Then encourage her to guess a number, and, if she's old enough, teach her why the best number would be either forty or forty-two (increases odds of winning). Let her count and see who wins. As you walk, point to a house with a house number posted and ask her what the number is.

HIDE AND SEEK: Always a favorite because of the action and drama involved. This game will also give you an opportunity to teach about clothes dryer safety, but don't do it the way Caleb did when Bullet (Caleb's cat) climbed into the clothes dryer and Caleb turned it on for a minute. Caleb told me that Bullet didn't go back to that side of the house for two years.

SPRAY BOTTLE GAME: Get a spray bottle that's not in use, fill it with water, give it to the child to go outside and spray six things — three things that begin with a *g*, three with a *t*, etc.

THE NO PLAN GAME: Give the kids a half day with no planned activities (especially if you're the type to plan tightly) and with plenty of fun things available like pots, pans, rocks, mud, sticks, stones, wheels off old things, shovels, sand, dirt, buckets.

FILL IN THE CIRCLES: Child fills in the loops on *p*'s and *o*'s in the newspaper. If that gets boring, then move on to *b*'s, *d*'s, and *q*'s, and capital *R*'s and *B*'s.

PUPPETS: Put socks on both your hands, turn a table onto its side, get behind it, and put the children on the other side. Let the socks rise just above the edge of the table and pretend the socks are two characters talking to each other. Then turn it all over to the kids, with guidance and suggestions, until they don't need them. When they're old enough, you can encourage them to write scripts.

OTHER GAMES FOR WHEN THEY'RE A LITTLE OLDER

READER'S THEATER: Take turns reading aloud from a favorite story while acting out parts. A more sophisticated method would be to make a script from a story. There could be speaking parts for characters as well as a part for a narrator who reads material between spoken parts. The staging, costuming, and audience could be as elaborate as desired. An alternative is to sit still and just read the parts. (Several ideas in this section of the book — including Reader's Theater and Lemons — come via my good friend and education professor mentor, Sterling Hennis.)

STORE: Place two dollars' worth of change on a table, "buy" items (pen, pencil, loaf of bread), pay the child (the store clerk), and ask for change. Play money or real money works. This might be an opportunity to talk about the 99 percent.

---

*C.O.D.

If you're a considerably older dad who grew up in the kind of close community I mentioned in the last C.O.D. and you also spent more time outdoors than kids tend to spend outdoors today, then you're lucky. You may have a solid feel for the reasons to get your kids outdoors and with other kids outdoors—on their own. We all remember childhood friends, but I feel particularly lucky for having been able to grow up in one community and remember it as if the community itself—the geography, farms, houses, filling station, grocery store, general store, grill, auto shop—were a valued relative, someone who sheltered me and showed me mysterious and welcoming places. To have that past is helpful in designing a present time for your kids. And with this background, you'll have stories about acquaintances, relatives, and places that cover decades. As a consequence of such stories, your children might feel a little more at home in the world.

LETTER GAME: On a car trip, see who can first find the alphabet in sequence, letter by letter, anywhere out there in the environment. A player must find an *A* before a *B* and a *B* before a *C,* and on through the alphabet. Road signs and license plates are prime sources. License plates are especially good for *X, Y,* and *Z.* Play individually or on teams.

HOMEWORK GAMES: Rather than asking your child to spell words aloud, you spell each word while giving your child an opportunity to say whether you are correct or incorrect (you spell, the child says true or false). You can use absurd spellings. This game can work with simple adding and subtracting problems, or in other subjects.

CARDS: An early card game, War — one you perhaps already know about — is fun at about the time a child is learning to count. Each player lays down a card, and the lower number is captured by the higher. Variations are endless — especially with the two colors, red and black.

---

*C.O.D.

You might identify with my somewhat off-the-subject ruminations on cards, mystery, God, and sex — just below.

People with power in earlier generations — on both sides of my family — outlawed cards in the home because of the sin of gambling. My parents allowed no cards in our house, thus creating suspense and mystery about them. This shows how norms (unwritten rules about what's appropriate and/or inappropriate in a time and place) can be formed in a home.

There was *not* in our home a lot of suspense and mystery about, say, God. He simply *was,* was not to be questioned, and He sat around every day with nothing much to do since He'd finished with creation and all that. He did listen to prayer and would *bust your ass* if you played cards. So cards were absent, mysterious, and forbidden, and God was clearly present, though invisible, and rather unmysterious. Thus cards stood—in some sense of significance, to me—oddly, about as big as God.

If cards had been as normal as waffles or plates and I'd been taught to count with them, then they would not have seemed so elevated. I mention this not so much to guide you, or reach conclusions myself, but to indicate the *continuing complexity of parenting and family norms.* (Not to speak of the continuing complexity of God.)

My parents taught about sex much like they taught about cards—they didn't talk about it. Consequently, sex became as big as cards, as mysterious, and to this day I consider my enjoyment of sex and cards, in part, as an unintended gift from my parents. (I had to sort of start over with God.)

Raising kids is more complicated than the stock market and the economics of the euro. Way more. For example, if my mother had spanked me for masturbating, then I might have been harmed in some way, but rather, she just warned me about it. I don't remember what she said exactly. (She'd never been exposed to "psychology" or formal education beyond sixth grade.) Because of this, I wasn't afraid of pain as a consequence of masturbation. I only had guilt to deal with. I had a vague sense that it was wrong. I didn't suffer shame, but more a kind of easy guilt that made the act interesting. And as Harry Crews quoted James Dickey, "Guilt is magic." Where does all this lead? I don't know. It's too deep for me.

Actually it leads to the fact that you may want your kids to internalize good and bad ways of behaving, thus experiencing guilt when they choose to do wrong. If you don't like the word *guilt,* then maybe *remorse* will work.

Many kids have bizarre guesses about what sex is all about. "A daddy gets a garden tool and plants a seed inside Mommy and it grows in her stomach and comes out her bottom as a watermelon and hurts a lot." The sense of wonder and enjoyment is often absent. A wise approach seems to be to let a child's questions lead to answers that help the child not become overwhelmed with information. Sex is a complicated subject, yet from some perspectives, very simple. There are tons of articles and websites and books giving specific advice on talking to your kid about sex. One thing is clear: the habit of conversing with and listening to your kid needs to be established before this or any other important topic is approached.

WACKY WORD GAME: Look at a newspaper ad, or even an obituary, and mark out each adjective, noun, number, and maybe a few adverbs. Let's say you've marked out an adjective, a noun, an adjective, another noun, an adverb, and a number in a short want ad. Ask the child for an adjective, write it down, then a noun, and so forth. Then read the ad with the child's words in place of the original words. You may need to explain adjective as "a describing word" and a noun as "a thing," but soon he'll begin learning the terminology.

MY GRANDMOTHER DROVE TO CALIFORNIA: The first player says, "My grandmother drove to California and in her trunk she took a(n) (adjective) (noun)."

Before you start playing, decide criteria for the noun: bigger than mountain or smaller than dinner plate, for example. Let's do nouns bigger than a mountain. First player says, "My grandmother drove to California and in her trunk she took a red sunset." Next player says, "My grandmother drove to California and in her trunk she took a red sunset and a big moon." Next player must add another adjective and noun after repeating all that's come before, including "My grandmother drove to California and in her trunk she took a..." If a player stumbles, others can help. There are no winners or losers. The journey is the destination.

. . . .

TWO AND A HALF YEARS OLD

Nathaniel,

About three inches of snow were on the ground at your grandparents' house and we'd borrowed a sled, one of those northern kinds, from next door, Sophia's house, and it was solid, one piece, wooden, with a curved front end, and I got you situated on the hill and got you started down a slope, aimed (I thought) through several trees — it was sort of open — but there was a tree about three or four inches in diameter down on the left, and the old sled just sort of started drifting that way and as I saw the sled was going to hit the tree, it started speeding up and you were sitting, perched, holding on with both hands and in the two seconds or so before impact I'm sure my mouth opened but I couldn't say anything...and then wham-wham—the first wham for the sled against the tree, and the second: your head against the tree. I started down, and slipped and fell, got up, got down there, happy in a way to hear you crying because I knew you were conscious. You were crying hard and you had a red scraped place above your right eye, and I picked you up and took you in and your mama held you for a long time and you cried and cried and cried, and I figure this may be one of your early memories.

Love,

Papadaddy

. . . .

COLLECTIONS ACTIVITIES: Go to junk shops and look for inexpensive things that a child has expressed an interest in collecting. Old cameras, fake diamonds, plastic horses, wooden blocks.

SPEAK/WRITE: Speak into an audio recorder. Each sentence must be five words long (or four or eight, etc.). Then listen back and write down the sentences. This gives parents a chance to help make writing fun.

BOOK MAKING: Child chooses a photo (digital or otherwise). Let the child say two sentences about the photo, and you write those underneath it (paste photo to sheet of paper — or just do all of this digitally). One photo with two sentences per page. Collect ten photos with sentences beneath and make into a book for the child to read. He should learn to see the words and say them, and this should be relatively easy since he recently came up with the words on his own. Ten of those books in a three-ring binder will make a 100-page book. All written by your son or daughter.

VACUUM CLEANER OVERHAUL: Well, maybe not a vacuum cleaner, but if you have an old computer and appropriate tools, or even an old talking toy and a hammer, your child may be interested in dismantling and putting back together the computer, or smashing the talking toy. While father/son, father/daughter construction projects are okay, some online experts describe elaborate father/son building projects almost as complicated as atom smashers that I'm guessing most boys wouldn't particularly enjoy if left to their own choices. It seems that many of these website-published projects are of the dads, by the dads, and for the dads. I'm guessing that in some cases, Junior can't wait to get to college.

LEMONS: This game requires more than a couple of players. So you might need to get neighborhood kids to join in. Everybody is given a lemon (or a leaf or a rock will work). Players spend time with their lemons — perhaps overnight. You cannot mark on your lemon. Get to know it, name it if you'd like, talk to it — but mainly memorize what it looks like. Take it with you to the bathroom, shopping, to the movies.

With all players present, the leader (you) takes up
the lemons (or leaves, etc.) and spreads them out
around the room. Then let players find their lemons.
This finding your lemon takes (trust me) no more than
thirty seconds. Now ask players to think about what
helped them find their lemons and ask them to write
a paragraph describing their lemons. After
descriptions are written, you take up the lemons
and place them about the room, in the hall, on
windowsills. Take up papers and redistribute them and
ask players to study the paper in front of them and
then take that paper and find the lemon it describes.
You say, "Put your paper under the lemon it
describes—*even if another paper is already under it.*"
After papers are placed under lemons, ask players to
find their lemons and the paper(s) under them. You

count the number of correct matches. If you want to keep going, you might help players discuss "description strategies" — obvious like color, shape, relative size, distinguishing marks, and less obvious like metaphors and similes (shaped like a pumpkin, as smooth as a baby's skin).

Players then make lemonade.

PLEASE/NO: This game needs several players also. One player says, "Please." Another says, "No." Observers suggest who the players might be and the topic under discussion, and then they may also suggest dialogue. The two role-players then come up with a conversation based on "Please/No." Players could write scripts to be acted out with sock puppets or with actors.

. . . .

FOUR YEARS OLD

Ridley,

We played touch football yesterday for the first time — your mother masterminded it, and then today I played you and Nathaniel and you-all beat me 24 to 6.

Love,

Papadaddy

. . . .

BOILERPLATE POETRY READING AND WRITING: Read the following poem aloud to your children.

Them Toad Suckers
by Mason Williams

How about them toad suckers, ain't they clods,
Sittin' there suckin' them green toady-frogs,
Suckin' them hop-toads, suckin' them chunkers,
Suckin' them leapy-types, suckin' them plunkers.
Look at them toad suckers, ain't they snappy,
Suckin' them bog-frogs, sure makes 'em happy.
Them hugger-mugger toad suckers, way down south,
Stickin' them sucky-toads in they mouth.
How to be a toad sucker, no way to duck it —
Get yourself a toad, rare back and suck it.

Kids will love the poem and ask you to read it over and over for the rest of your life. Use this form as a boilerplate for poetry they can write out.

How about them _____, ain't they _____,
Sittin' there _____in' them _____,
Etc.

A classic blues format also works well for writing poems or songs:

I went down to the river yesterday afternoon
I went down to the river yesterday afternoon
When I got down to the river
I went fishing
Etc.

FILMMAKING AND PODCASTS: Children write scripts, rehearse, and produce their own films or podcasts. A secret is to have no video or audio recording over seven minutes long and have a "director" who is responsible for the final product.

IN THE MANNER OF THE ADVERB: A player leaves the room, and those remaining in the room pick any adverb — often an *ly* word. Let's say the word is "slowly." Keep it secret; invite player back into room. Let that player watch as a leader says to a player (who was in the room and knows the adverb; let's say, Jack), "Move a chair, Jack, in the manner of the adverb." Jack moves the chair from one place to another, slowly. Then the leader says to another player who knows the word, "Pick up that pencil [or something else] in the manner of the adverb." The player picks up a pencil slowly. Anytime the player who earlier left the room wants to guess, she guesses what she thinks the adverb is. Then another game with another adverb and a different guesser. No winners — the journey is the...

PART THREE

LATER ON

Preparations

BE PREPARED FOR

A trip to the movies with your child and his/her friend after which you buy them each a chocolate milkshake. Your child's friend throws up her milkshake onto your child and the backseat of your car.

HOW TO PREPARE

Keep a roll of paper towels in any vehicle you own.

BE PREPARED FOR

Your four-year-old son will poop big-time in his blue jeans and down his leg while you're in a grocery story with him, your wife, and your three-year-old daughter. You will volunteer to stay with your daughter while your wife takes your son to the bathroom — back in there where all the extra bread and veggies are stored.

Your wife says, "Come on back, I might need you."

You follow them back with younger daughter in tow. You're hoping nobody's in the bathroom back there. Bathrooms in the back of grocery stores are usually unpeopled, as they are out of sight of patrons. (Who wants to sell bread from beside the men's room?) You and your little daughter follow through wide, swinging doors that lead to the storage area. The women's room is locked. Your wife goes into the men's room with your son. Your job is to guard the door. You can't see what is happening in there, but you later learn that after undressing and cleaning him up as much as she can, your wife decides to throw away his underpants. That's when he starts screaming about his underwear being thrown away. When he starts screaming, a man who is bigger than you walks up to you and says, "Are you waiting?" You say, "No, but my wife is in there with my son." He looks at your daughter as if to say, "I think your father's a liar." You think about going into the bathroom to help, but you don't especially want to take your daughter in there, with the screaming and all, and you don't want to leave your daughter by herself while you go in to help. You then realize that you should be the one in there, not your wife. A woman comes out of the ladies' room, and you say to the guy standing there, "Maybe you could use the women's bathroom," and he says, "No."

Your son is still screaming and the man says, "Jesus Christ." He starts into the men's room. This is when a lot of things are going through your mind.

HOW TO PREPARE

Keep a change of your children's clothes and a roll of paper towels in any vehicle you own.

Miscellaneous

LICE

When you answer a call on your cell phone from a teacher or a counselor or your wife that your child has head lice, the conversation will start like this: "Are you sitting down?" And then after you hear that your child has lice, you will wonder what the big deal is, and you'll wonder again when you see your child and she and her hair look all normal. Your wife will hand you a sheet of paper from the school with a letter on one side and advice on the other. She will then leave for her uncle's home in Tampa, Florida.

The advice on the back of the letter will seem too troublesome to follow, so you'll find and follow a less troublesome set of instructions on the web. This advice will have you washing all the clothes, furniture, bed linens, and books in your home, twice. This less troublesome set of instructions will also ask you to vacuum your yard and the roof of your home as well as the inside of your toilet. After three days and your child still has lice, you will follow the *more* troublesome advice found on the Internet and in letters from your school and your church's day-care facility. When *that* advice doesn't work and you find that lice have spread to a second child, consider the following:

1. Burn down your home and move into another that's at least six miles away.

2. Since your child will have run back into the burning house and saved each of her two hundred individually named stuffed animals, you will have to wash each one of those, separately, twice, in lye soap and rubbing alcohol and then shrink-wrap them and store them in sealed plastic bags inside sealed plastic jugs in a large rented freezer for two years. Shrink-wrap the freezer.

3. Buy fifty gallons of vinegar. This will be cheaper than many products sold for lice removal. White vinegar is preferred, but any will do as long as it has 5 percent acidity. Buy a snorkel and mask for your child, pour the vinegar into a tub, and leave your child submerged for four to seven hours. You must hold your child's head so that the hair remains under vinegar and the end of the snorkel above vinegar. If your wife is back from Tampa, which she probably won't be, you can exchange head-holding duties with her on the hour. Your child will become a pickle for a few days.

There is an alternative method for getting rid of lice. Rather than the burn-your-home-then-child-in-the-tub treatment, you examine each hair on your child's head with the Hubble telescope fitted with a special lice attachment. You will see that the egg of a louse looks like a teeny, tiny drop of water. Remove it with a blowtorch. You protect your child's head with a thick coating of axle grease or nonflammable mayonnaise prior to blowtorching.

So far we've not mentioned the actual lice themselves. We've not discussed what a louse looks like or how to kill it. I'm forbidden to do either because my lawyer is now in negotiation with two of them at an undisclosed location.

A good website is headlicecenter.com.

BIRTHDAY PARTIES
(say, the ninth)

Two types of birthday parties, Type X and Type Y:

TYPE X. Some parents tend to give their children birthday parties that go something like this. The parents:

- Send out invitations to 160 kids.
- Rent a state park.
- Have a roller skating rink moved in.
- Order eighty pizzas (forty plain cheese and forty pepperoni).
- Rent a couple of those bouncy platforms with roof and walls wherein children can go crazy jumping up and down while hitting smaller children in the face. (They get away with this meanness because the smaller children will not leave the tent and go tell their parents what just happened because they are having so much fun jumping.)
- Rent a water slide.
- Order an ice cream truck—for the children to drive around in the state park after eating all the ice cream.
- Hire a clown, not knowing he's a sex offender in four southern states.
- Buy a very large cake made for the occasion, with those funny candles that won't blow out.
- Buy a pony for their child.
- Set aside three hours (just after the published time for parents to pick up their children) for the opening of presents by the birthday child.

Cost: $12,000–$14,000

A major consequence: six parents experience rageful impatience while the birthday child opens presents.

TYPE Y. The parents of the child's three best friends bring them to the birthday child's house one hour before school on the child's birthday. A parent takes the four children to a Waffle House or a similar diner for breakfast and lets them sit together in a booth while the parent sits at the counter.

Cost: $27

A major consequence: a peaceful time for the parent to look over a newspaper left on the counter and eat a good breakfast. The child and friends are ecstatic and have an opportunity to talk to one another.

FAMILY VISITS

Every other summer or so, go with your child or children to visit one great-aunt, great-uncle, grandmother, grandfather — *with an audio or video recorder.* Collect family stories. Don't ask Grandma general questions; rather, ask her specific questions, like "Grandma, do you remember a path that led from your house to somewhere else?"

"Oh yes. There was. Let's see. It led to the old house spring. I'd kind of forgotten that."

"Who went there and what did you and they do?"

Look for some dirt, unless it's too plentiful already. Do your job with that recorder—this summer or during a summer when your child gets old enough to enjoy collecting stories. Your children will cling to and love stories about grandparents, great-grandparents, you, and themselves. Write those stories down or otherwise record, then retell them. Don't allow their loss. How sad that the stories of Disney et al. may tend to replace our own.

FOOD

If you put cabbage on a kid's plate for thirty-three days in a row, then the child will begin to eat it somewhere in the twenty-five-day range. Or so I've read—or maybe it wasn't quite like that. Also, if you're sure he eats fruit every day, you can worry less about vegetables, so I've heard—this may help you relax if one of your children won't eat veggies.

The important interval for checking the amount of food consumed by a child is not from the beginning of one meal until the end of that meal, nor is it from morning till night. What you want to check, in case you're worried, is how much he's eating in a week.

When Caleb sits down at the table with his kids, he says: "If you don't see it, you don't need it."

Professional parenting people will suggest that you never

relate food to punishment or reward. It's highly symbolic to a young child and can cause resentment. That makes sense to me.

WHaT a PLate oF VegetaBLes LooKs LiKe to A KiD

HOLIDAY SHOPPING

I've learned to do most of my holiday shopping at the local hardware store. Wonderful possibilities there. For Mama, too. And any place that sells local honey is a good bet for gift shopping.

. . . .

THIRTEEN DAYS OLD

Nathaniel,

About a week ago I went for a walk in the big field (where I first shot at a covey of quail with Daddy many years ago), and it was about May 15 and the day seemed perfect. It was a mild day, but there were pockets of cool, almost cold, air that I could walk through and that felt very good, there in this field that once belonged to my granddaddy, and there were buttercups and purple wildflowers all in the field, and I was walking along a mowed path, and the presence of the cool air, my knowing I had a good family nearby — all this made me very happy.

Love,
Daddy

- -

*C.O.D.

It's not easy sometimes. I'm speaking of being a dad, young or old. There will be times you want to be alone. There will be times you want to be with your buddies. But if you're older and in excellent health, your buddies will start dying, and that option of being with them will be gone. (Remember, on the day you're born, and on every day afterward, your age group gets smaller.) And as an older dad, you'll get time with energetic young people who are parents of your children's friends.

Of course, it's not guaranteed that you'll be in excellent health. But the need to be all there to take care of and play with your youngins will be a good incentive for staying in shape. Fatherhood-later-in-life produces a secret, good chemical.

when I was your age all I needed was a rock, but kids these days are all about sticks. I don't get it.

OLD-TIMER, 5000 B.C.

SPORTS

It's hard for me to justify making a kid play any sport or be a Boy Scout or do any of those activities unless he's really motivated. I've watched too many kids adopt the survival-of-the-fittest mentality of their fathers—in some cases, mothers. We're familiar with the stories of Little League parents who are far more involved with kids' ball games than the kids want to be.

I remember the joy of being on a ball field, playing baseball, for summers and summers and summers — without adults nearby. I also played organized ball, but I remember the unsupervised play just as fondly, if not more so.

Consider letting them play what they want to play.

Or *not* play "your" sport. I was proud that my older daughter chose to play baseball, and I was just as proud — and somehow relieved — many years later, when I saw one of my sons, on being told he would have to sit on the bench for a few innings, pump his fist and whisper *yes*. He was not buying into a racket that wasn't his.

KIDS' JOURNALS

Until they are willing to write in them themselves, you can transcribe what kids have to say into their journals. You might establish journaling as a norm by keeping one yourself. A child's journal offers opportunities for the child to write about her emotions — write about something that makes her angry, sad, or happy. "We had to take Joey to the vet and he was put to sleep. I was very sad. Daddy does not seem so sad."

FAMILY MEETINGS

Once, my two boys (then ages five and three) were up after their bedtime in a vacation house. They left their room, visited a bathroom in the house, and squirted perfume on each other. The next morning we had a little family meeting.

We sat on the floor in a circle, I with my back to the wall.

After establishing some new clear rules and expectations, I asked if anybody had something to say. Kristina added her important perspective. Our one-and-a-half-year-old daughter was also at the meeting. This was a serious meeting, somber tone, etc. I asked if anyone else wanted to speak. Our younger son, Ridley, said, "I do." I moved over and gave him the speaker's place — his back to the wall. He looked around. I said, "Go ahead." He hesitated, smiling. I said, "Go ahead." He looked around the circle at each of us and then said, "Poopy butt."

Freedom of speech is important, and a structured time and place for kids to practice it in the family helps them experience a healthy childhood.

EARPLUGS

Always keep them handy. Use them while driving, but if you stop the car on a railroad track to eat celery sticks and peanut putter, or potato chips, remove them from your ears.

PART FOUR

The Long View and Avoiding Factor Bad

Some kids Never change

OVERVIEW

My job as we come down the final stretch in this book is to suggest how you might avoid certain situations as your child transitions into young adulthood. I will *not* suggest how you might get your child to become a certain kind of person — because we may hope for different outcomes. Some of us want our child to be a quiet mathematician, and some are hoping for a lively and talkative avant-garde abstract painter, and some of us are hoping for a calm tightrope walker or a bluegrass mandolin player. Most of us, of course, will not think so much about the distant future, about specific occupations, but will want to concentrate on assisting our children in their experiencing a full, uninterrupted childhood — that springtime we discussed earlier — so that they will be happy and fruitful as they move on through summer, fall, and winter (finally without us) choosing what they want to do with their lives and/or end up with as an obsession.

In the following section I'll suggest something I think you don't want. In the section after that, Concepts and Tests, I'll give you some perhaps not-so-familiar terms to think through, and then, finally, I'll suggest how to increase chances of avoiding certain "Factor Bads."

What Could Happen
Down the Line and Why

MOTORCYCLE GANG

Let's say that at midnight one Saturday night your seventeen-year-old drives a Harley-Davidson motorcycle onto your front lawn while holding, speared onto the end of a long stick, an object that resembles a scalp. About a dozen other riders are in attendance—each with his or her motorcycle and object on a stick. This child—your daughter—yells out, "Daddy." She is intoxicated and naked, as are the others.

You walk out onto the porch and think, This is not what I'd hoped for.

The above scenario may *not* be your vision of your worst nightmare—especially if you are in a motorcycle club (or gang) and enjoy outdoor sports and relaxation and you are a member of some kind of fringe nudist militia. And if this is not your worst nightmare about your child's young adulthood, then substitute something that is—we'll call it "Factor Bad."

I want to help you avoid Factor Bad. But I'll not give directions like many parenting books: "If you do A, B, and C, you get good result D." Applied to humans, many systematic technologies (good for building cars and toasters the same way every time) fail because they lack "dither." Dither makes room for our differences, helps us embrace uncertainty once in a while.

I'm going to try to give you a head start on avoiding that rumble out in the front yard, or some other Factor Bad.

SEVERAL POSSIBLE ORIGINS OF A FACTOR BAD

1. I recently saw a father standing under an umbrella at our elementary school waiting for his daughter in a chilly rain. His daughter ran to him and they talked under the umbrella. She had on a short-sleeved blouse. I could hear the father's words but not hers.

   "You don't have your jacket?"

   Some discussion followed.

   "Where's your jacket?"

   Some discussion.

   "Do you want to go back and get it?"

   Discussion.

   "I'll walk with you. Or do you want to go on home? Do you want to go home or do you want to go back in and get your jacket?"

   I wanted to shout: "She's five years old. Go get the jacket—or don't go get the jacket. Just say, 'Let's go get your jacket' or 'Let's go home.'" Was I watching an adult unable to make a decision because of "respect for a child," a fear of "getting it wrong"?

2. Accepting a "no" from a small child after a reasonable request of that child can be dangerous to the world. A

small child's small brain is not ready for certain kinds of judgment. Hell, young people are still learning how to make judgments in their early twenties. You are a provider of firm, fair walls as well as a provider of opportunity.

3. "Let's go to bed. *OKAY?*" The one-word parental *question* "Okay?" tells a kid who is in charge, who is controlling the situation. You probably don't want a child controlling those situations that you need to control. Children often need clear direction, structure, and limits. When a father is afraid of making his child unhappy and thus asks the child to make some kind of decision, like "Well, Johnny, would you like to go to bed or stay up?" because sending the child to bed will make him unhappy, then the father, in a few years, may be taking directions from a worried, impatient, frowning, unsteady child—unsteady because he's not sure what kind of important decision he may be asked to make next. He is very clear that he need not tolerate being told what to do. At some point around age five, he starts thinking, "Motorcycle." "Scalp." He's aging too fast, missing out on the springtime of life—a full childhood.

On the other hand, a child of course needs to begin to learn how to make decisions. I hope you'll handle choice making sensibly. For example, if your child likes to play with old pots and pans in the backyard, as many children do, you might offer seven pans to the child and ask him to pick five of those to play with. (This child is just learning to count.) The child will be happy but is being granted a brand of power that does not endanger his health—as staying up all night might. Now, if you offer your child this pots-and-pan choice and he throws a temper tantrum because he wants to play with all the pots and pans—well...I deal with temper tantrums down below, but I'm thinking if your wife has still not returned from Tampa (regarding the lice problem), you might want to call a relative who is strict but not too strict to come stay with your child for a year and feed the dog and goldfish while you go join your wife. You'll have those days.

I don't know how fathers stay in marriages with mamas who allow the child to do only what the child wants to do — or stay in marriages with mamas who, on the other hand, rule with iron fists. I'm extraordinarily lucky to live with a wife who believes in the middle road. You can do worse, in looking for literature about raising children, than buying *Poor Richard's Almanack.*

4) When Caleb goes into a store with his kids, Holden and Lila, he points to a wall just inside of the door and says, "Sit." They sit against the wall. Then he says, "Stay." When anybody asks Caleb why his kids mind so well, he says it's because he uses the book *Water Dog,* by Richard A. Wolters, to train them. Disclosure: Caleb is made up, though at least one of my friends will be asking for money because he thinks I'm writing about him. I'm not altogether sure if Caleb is a source of, or cure for, Factor Bads. So much has to do with tone.

WHAT BEHAVIORS DO YOU LEAVE ALONE?

Masturbation.

I'm suggesting you leave that alone — except for answering any and all questions your child asks about sex.

So, what other parts of "kids will be kids" behavior do you leave alone? Or not leave alone? These are questions with no easy answer.

Here's an example: your doorbell, assuming you have one, will be rung over and over by your kids and that may be the kind of thing that will not bother you, but if you're like me it will drive you crazy and you must decide what part of that kind of behavior to swallow, what part to prohibit. Now, I'm not talking about a kid walking up and ringing the doorbell *once* every few days. I'm talking about a child standing in front of the doorbell pressing the button over and over and over, one time after another (normal child behavior): Ring Ring Ring Ring Ring Ring Ring Ring Ring Ring Ring Ring Ring Ring Ring Ring Ring Ring Ring Ring Ring Ring Ring Ring Ring Ring Ring Ring Ring Ring Ring Ring Ring Ring Ring Ring Ring Ring Ring Ring Ring Ring Ring Ring Ring Ring Ring Ring Ring Ring Ring Ring Ring Ring Ring Ring Ring Ring while you're sitting on the commode, or maybe you're on the phone, or under the bed painting the support slats. (Consider removing before painting.)

When you get to the door and you look at your smiling child, you might feel guilty about your anger and say, "Please don't do that any more."

It's this kind of annoying childlike behavior — you have your own examples, or you will, unless you're now in Tampa — that I have generally become, or tried to become, more tolerant of with each successive child, and this added tolerance may help explain why psychologists say that the younger children in a family are often a little more relaxed and easygoing than the older ones.

So we have that nebulous category of the doorbell-ringing variety of behavior — how best to respond is not always clear. But if the kids are feeding poison to the hamster or shooting BB guns at neighbors, then a firm and controlled demonstration of anger and astonishment might be a deterrent that works until you can get at some underlying problems in the *relationship* of your child with you and your wife and the world. That "relationship" — and the vocabulary that will be useful in discussing it — is what I'll cover below, especially in the next section: CONCEPTS AND TESTS.

AS WE ENCOURAGE AND RESTRICT BEHAVIOR, WHAT ARE WE SAYING?

Any reward and punishment behavior from you (random, with warning, without warning, mood related, too early, too late, harsh, lax, etc.) teaches a child:

- What *you*, the father, value in terms of right and wrong.
- What you believe about fair play (or justice) as shown by your actions.
- What behavioral norms you value, consciously and unconsciously (TV, snacking, church, lying, bullying, passivity, noise, silence, kindness). (Therefore *your child may have a tendency to value those whether he realizes it or not.*)

If your child knows that you are trying to be fair and are willing to apologize if you think you've been unfair, and if the child has plenty of examples of your fairness, then the relationship you have in place has a good chance of working for positive outcomes. When will you know it didn't work? When you hear the rumble on the lawn.

"GIFTED" CHILDREN CAN BECOME
GIFTED BUMS

A few days ago I read a *New York* magazine article, "How Not to Talk to Your Kids" (nymag.com/news/features/27840/), by Po Bronson. The article proposes that children will perform better if you suggest they've "worked hard" on a project (if they have) than if you tell them they are "smart" or "gifted." This dichotomy is of course a bit more complicated than that, but the article made an impression on me.

(Here's a good chance to make an important point. The above paragraph assumes something. It assumes our children listen to us and care about what we say. They will listen to us and care about what we say if we're in the home a good bit of the time, looking them in the eye, and listening to what they say. My general assumption is that if you're reading this book — rather than playing golf or sitting in an office somewhere obsessing over a "portfolio" — you are or will be that kind of father.)

A main idea of the article is that kids who have been told, and believe, that they are smart, tend to also believe, when they find a task difficult, that the difficulty is not their problem. Since they are smart, they should be able to perform the task, and since they can't perform it, why try? Or if they try and fail, someone may suddenly consider them "not very smart." They don't want that.

Kids who learn that success comes from sticking with a problem are less likely than their "gifted" counterparts to give up. Here's a short quote pulled from the article:

According to a survey conducted by Columbia University, 85 percent of American parents think it's important to tell their kids that they're smart....The constant praise is meant to be an angel on the shoulder, ensuring that children do not sell their talents short.

But a growing body of research—and a new study from the trenches of the New York public-school system—strongly suggests it might be the other way around. Giving kids the label of "smart" does not prevent them from underperforming. It might be causing it.

The article also suggests that students considering themselves gifted tend to cheat more than others.

Because research studies are often flawed and tend to support the beliefs of their creators, I try to not rely on them too heavily, but this particular article was convincing and has changed the way I verbally praise and challenge my children—in the last few days I've probably been overplaying it a bit, but I'll calm down over time.

Concepts and Tests

WALLS

Your children will bump against those firm walls you provide for them. They will also run through spaces where no walls stand. Those existing, firm walls may keep your children from harming themselves physically and from becoming emotionally unmoored. Finding the threshold to "too much freedom" is important. If you were granted sensible sets of freedoms and limits in your own childhood, you'll probably do well in this important fathering quality.

Test:

Q. If your child wants to run across a busy interstate highway, do you stop him even if it means holding him on the ground?

A. Yes.

Q. If your eighteen-year-old daughter wants to marry Jerry Lee Lewis, do you allow her to do so?

A. Probably not.

Q. If your thirty-year-old daughter wants to marry a toy-advertising executive, do you allow her?

A. No.

NORMS

A mentor of mine, Phil Schlechty (schlechtycenter.org), told me this story from his early days of teaching sociology:

Beginning of the semester, Educational Sociology class, Phil stands in front of the class and starts out by asking, "Any questions?"

Silence.

He says, "See you next time" and walks out.

Second class he opens by asking, "Any questions?"

Silence.

He says, "Be sure to come back next time" and walks out.

Third class, he opens his lecture by asking, "Any questions?" Silence. He pulls off his shirt, places it on the lectern, walks over, opens a window (first floor) and jumps out, walks back into class, puts his shirt back on, and says, "Any questions?"

Someone asks, "Why did you do that?"

He then starts his first lecture. Topic: norms. The lecture starts something like this:

"Let me ask you to think about every high school and college class—or just about every one—you've ever had. My guess is that no teacher ever said, 'Don't ask questions at the beginning of the class.' Yet *Don't ask questions at the beginning of a class* is a norm—an unwritten rule about what's appropriate in a given situation. It's invisible and rarely, if ever, stated. Yet it's powerful and somehow applied *consistently*. This norm about no questions is so powerful I could count on it being very difficult to break. I had to break a professor norm—don't jump out a classroom window with your shirt off—in order to increase chances of a student norm being broken while I make a point in an abnormal way."

Because they will not likely go anywhere in a car without wearing one, your children will accept the wearing of seat belts as a norm. Every time you drive away from home, you require your children to wear seat belts. Think about how effective norms are. But they are sometimes hard to establish. My younger children are nine, seven, and six as I write this, and I ask them over and over to not ring the doorbell. But they ring it over and over. I ask them over and over to put their shoes where they can find them the next morning, but over and over I find myself asking, "Where are your shoes?" I've somehow not been consistent or effective in norm setting. Yet when I get in the car, I say nothing and they buckle up. The norm was established early in their lives. Clearly, *consistency of application* is behind the effectiveness of many norms. My children know their set bedtime. They expect to go to bed at the same time every night. Kristina and I have managed to set a norm. This ain't going to last, I'm sure, but right now it's working.

This business of norms is so important to fathering, and norm application so obvious, I think I can go straight to the test.

Test:

Q. Your child pees in the yard before bedtime each night. How did this become a norm?

A. Your own father started it, and then you didn't know your son was watching *you* all those times.

VARIABLE-RATIO REINFORCEMENT

What if every once in a while, you said, "On this car trip, no seat belts required." Then, after that, say the third or fifth or second time (in a given week) that you get into your car with your children and they ask if they can *roam free in the car without a seat belt,* you say, "Sure." At other times when they ask for this freedom, you say, "No. You must wear your seat belt." And you make them wear their seat belts on those occasions.

You've set up a situation where they'll be asking ALL THE TIME to get out of that awful seat belt. That's because *a variable-ratio reinforcement* is in effect — *an extraordinarily strong schedule of reinforcement.* In spite of a "rule" against it, every once in a while the children get what they want. Let's take a somewhat different situation: if, very predictably, on every fifth time they ask to roam free in the car, you say "Sure," then you have a consistent ratio of reinforcement, and that nonvarying ratio would encourage them to keep asking but with less hope for success than with that variable-ratio schedule (fifth, second, third, fourth, ninth, etc.).

In establishing children's bedtimes, if you are as consistent as you must be with a seat belt (zero exceptions), you'll probably eventually experience somewhat similar results — compliance with little or no fuss. *It's that variable-ratio reinforcement that can work against you powerfully.* I'm suggesting here that if you understand the variable-ratio reinforcement and its bad consequences, and the power of *consistency* in establishing norms, you're less likely to go crazy and may reduce chances of a Factor Bad down the line.

Test:

Q. If you give your child dessert *before* a meal twice a year, is this enough to be considered a use of variable-ratio reinforcement, even if the child didn't ask for dessert on those occasions?

A. Maybe, and if you are an older dad, don't take chances. Enjoy life. Always eat your dessert first.

. . . .

TWENTY-ONE MONTHS OLD

Truma,

Yesterday we anchored the boat in shallow water in a quiet place, and then while eating lunch, burritos, you flipped right out of the boat, amazing, and I jumped in and got you out of the water. My sandals got stuck in the mud but I saved them. My cell phone got wet though. You were squalling but got okay. You're at the stage where you're very smart and don't know a lot of words (but quite a few) and so you whine right often just like the boys (and we all) did/do. We got three chickens yesterday: Snowball, Redbird, and Freckles. Pretty dramatic. They take care of themselves really well.

Love,

Papadaddy

. . . .

EXTINGUISHING BEHAVIOR
THROUGH IGNORING

If you ignore certain child behaviors enough times in a row, extinction of that behavior may follow. Some parenting experts are big on this. Some don't like it. But for this technique to work, the ignoring has to be *complete* (and the ignored behavior should not of course be harmful to the child). However, if you ignore certain behaviors of your spouse or in-laws, those behaviors will increase until they get what they want, or you die.

This one is kind of tough. You don't want to be ignoring behaviors of a kid who's smart enough to figure things out. At a certain age, let's say two, you can ignore temper tantrums, let's say nineteen in a row, and after that you may never see another one because the kid stopped getting what he was getting: *a certain kind of attention.*

But when the child gets a little older, say three and a half, and is drinking your whiskey and you decide to extinguish that behavior by ignoring it, you might have a problem. What might happen if you ignore this behavior is your son will invite his friends over for whiskey.

Early tantrums can be ignored consistently with a chance that you'll extinguish the behavior. But the reason they're happening is probably because they've been successful for the child.

The sad fact is that the time between your child's being too ignorant to figure out you're extinguishing certain behaviors through ignoring and the time he'll be ecstatic that you're ignoring is about six weeks.

OVERHEARD BABY CONVERSATION
ABOUT TANTRUMS

BABY 1: How about them temper tantrums — do they
work for you?

BABY 2: Oh yes. Big time. Just about every time.
Especially when I get kind of bluish red in the
face and scream. I just need to be sure Mommy
and Daddy, like, know what I want. Like it's
especially a good way to get candy, dude,
because candy is always around and all they
have to do is hand it to me and suddenly the
room is quiet and they can get back to
whatever they were doing. My tantrums, like,
work best when we're around other people, say,
at somebody's house or in a store somewhere or,
like, at the country club pool. My parents can't
stand for anything in our family to look out of
line. We live in a gated community.

If you ignore temper tantrums (or other behavior you
wish to extinguish), you will find that *if* the ignored behaviors were *not* ignored for a while, then they will get lots
worse while being ignored and then finally they will most
likely fade if the ignoring is *consistent*. Of course, if your
wife or somebody else is allowing the child to get what he
wants during or just after a temper tantrum, then your
ignoring will probably not work.

Now, depending on the severity of the tantrum, you can
sometimes successfully pick up the toddler who is having a

temper tantrum or just crying with frustration, walk to the window, and say, "Let's see if we can find Mr. Squirrel!" Then you get *really* excited and say, "Is he up in that *tree?*...Is he behind that *bush?*" With some luck, the child's head is turning from tree to bush and he's definitely into looking for that squirrel. Sometimes there may even be a squirrel. I've been lucky in this regard—very few temper tantrums (so far) and our youngest is six. I try to model, discuss, and demonstrate other ways of getting attention when unhappy. We do some role-playing sometimes—act out the right way to ask for something and then the wrong way. For example, at the dinner table in our kitchen, my wife or I may announce that we are at that moment eating dinner at Mrs. Smith's house. The children know that this calls for especially good manners—which they've been taught, thanks to Mom. After doing that for two minutes or so, they may sometimes have a minute at Mrs. Wigglebottoms's house, where just about anything goes. Elbows come onto the table, fingers pick up food, and they may talk with their mouths full.

. . . .

SIX YEARS OLD

Nathaniel,
    Tonight you had a temper tantrum at dinner
(you've had maybe three in your six years) because
you weren't allowed to have dessert (because you
didn't eat supper), and after you came out of time-out
you had another tantrum because Cousin yelled at
you, and I asked you to come to your room and you

were screaming and I tried what I've heard is a good idea. I said, "Let me hold you, Bud." Then I held you. And you let me. I was a little surprised. Then I held both your hands as we talked and you were sort of squeezing my hands while you still cried and were upset, and then I asked you to take three deep breaths but you didn't want to and you wanted to go back out but I said I didn't think you were ready, that you needed to calm down before going back. You took three very quick breaths and started back out to the living room and I told you you weren't ready and you went to the bathroom, came back and swatted at me in an unconscious, almost friendly way and took three breaths again. Then you were fine. It was a good exchange. Later, when I read your good night story, you put your head on my shoulder. And you're turning into one heck of a good reader.

Love,

Papadaddy

. . . .

Test:

Q. If you ignore a temper tantrum sixteen times in a row and your child has another temper tantrum because he wants a bag of peanuts and you give him the peanuts to get him quiet, will the sixteen times of ignoring be lost?

A. Yes. It will now take about thirty-two times of ignoring. Build a tree house. You can go there while the child is having a temper tantrum and your spouse is ignoring it.

THE SELFISH GENE

UCPs or Unselfish Cave People were some of the most fun and enjoyable and carefree people you can imagine. Big tribes of them were all over the place several million years ago.

They were killed out by SFEs or Survival of the Fittest Enthusiasts, and so what's left is a dominant selfish gene in all children. When your child is four or so (maybe three), you can start discussing with him the subject of selfishness, how it can be good and bad, how it can set a negative tone in the house, and you can model ways of behaving unselfishly. (But remember that that gene is legitimately present in the system.)

Contributing to religious or other charities might help demonstrate what you're after, and role-playing can help lead to discussions. (I'm serious here.) Sit in a real or make-believe wheelchair, tell the children you can't talk, that you are an older man named Bart and that you need food and shelter. See what they do. (Don't say that Bart has lice in his hair.)

You or someone else can also role-play a millionaire in a desk chair behind a desk. The millionaire (or billionaire) writes commercials played on TV to children. Place a plastic tarp on the floor beneath him and hang one behind him and throw tomatoes and eggs at him. This teaches intolerance for greedy people. You can discuss greed of this sort as up against the greed we use to survive. It's fascinating to read evolutionary science explanations of why we are some of the ways we are.

Follow up role-playing with discussion and suggestions from the children about further role-playing.

Test:

Q. Where can you get a wheelchair?
A. From one of the older dads.

THE SIMPLE THEORY I: FULL CHILD / CLIENT CHILD / PRODUCT CHILD

Phil Schlechty, the Educational Sociology professor who jumped out the classroom window, came up with a way of looking at educator-student relationships that are useful in talking about parenting roles. (I will be oversimplifying somewhat. At the same time, unfamiliar terms may induce you to come up with your own terms.)

Schlechty feels that an educator tends to see students in certain ways. *Students may be seen as:*

- Full Members: having some say in what happens to them (or)
- Clients: having no say, but with certain individual needs that school attempts to meet (or)
- Products: having no say, but with similar needs, thus treated the same

The educator behaves toward students in large part according to how he sees them. Let's draw a parallel by saying the father's behavior toward the child is closely related to *how the father sees the child*. These father categories will parallel the three educator categories just above. (Stay with me.)

The father *sees the child* as one of the following:

- Full Child: giving and receiving child
  (or)
- Client Child: a child with little or no voice and only certain needs to be filled
  (or)
- Product Child: a child with no voice who is to be controlled

Clearly the above categories can overlap, but I'm going for a helpful simplicity here. The father's relationship with his child and his resulting behavior is based in large part on how he generally *sees the child*.

Let me go a little further with the educator/father analogy. Another part of our system is how the child sees herself, and here I'll use Schlechty's student terms to suggest how your child might see herself.

THE SIMPLE THEORY II: NORMATIVE / CALCULATIVE / ALIENATED

Normative View

The child with this self view fully accepts and believes in (internalizes) unwritten rules about what's appropriate (i.e., norms) that the parents wish the child to accept.

Calculative View

The child with this self view thinks, "If I do A, maybe I can get B—what I want," and behaves accordingly.

Alienated View

The child is unwilling to accept any limits on behavior offered by the parents. The child wants nothing to do with the parents.

THE SIMPLE THEORY III: STRATEGIES

Now we have both father and child behaving according to how the child is "seen" and "sees herself." If you will accept that a person generally learns from his or her own behavior and its consequences, we can now set up a little formula, where FB is Father Behavior and CB is Child Behavior:

$$FB \rightarrow CB \rightarrow Learning$$

The formula says that Father Behavior influences Child Behavior and Child Behavior leads to Learning. (We could just as easily be using PB, Parent Behavior, for FB, Father Behavior.)

So far, so good. Clearly, if the child is treated as a product, she'll tend to become alienated, and if she's accepted fully, she'll be apt to accept the father's unwritten rules, or norms. But in the real world something else is going on.

$FB \longleftrightarrow CB \rightarrow Learning$. Father's Behavior doesn't just influence Child's Behavior; Child's Behavior influences Father's Behavior at the same time. This formula could keep on expanding, but for our purposes it stops here. It's meant to be a little model that helps us think about important aspects of fathering.

In an ideal world, we'd find the father seeing his child as a full child and the child accepting parental norms. Probably closer to the average relationship is a father seeing the child kind of like a client with needs, and the child becoming calculative. (Calculative behavior is of course quite normal in all of us.)

The father is always influencing the child, and vice versa, but the father is generally in the driver's seat. The above terms and descriptions call for father *strategies* to make things work the best way. Here are three such strategies.

Full Strategy

I, the father, consider what the child is most likely thinking and why, and I honor that thinking as I influence desired behavior in ways I think are fair to the child and to me.

Exchange Strategy

I buy the child's behavior that I want.

Coercive Strategy

The child must do A, no matter what, or else...so I coerce the child to behave in a certain way.

Now. Let's say a child rings the doorbell ten times in quick succession.

CASE A. The father says, "Stop it or I'll whip your ass." This is a kind of coercive strategy that may *alienate* the child, and this is more likely to happen when the child is seen as *product* than when seen in other ways.

You're probably ahead of me: using a full strategy with an alienated child won't work. We may have to work over time toward balance and desired outcomes. For example, we might need some exchange strategy scaffolding for a while.

CASE B. The father says, "Stop ringing the doorbell and I'll let you play with my cell phone." Here's an exchange strategy that may generate a *calculative* attitude in the child who is seen as a *client* (with a need, in this case, to manipulate something, the doorbell or a cell phone).

CASE C. The father first talks to the child, explains what happens to him (the father) when the doorbell keeps ringing. The father also recognizes out loud while talking that the child must want to make magic noise, and then gives the child a bell (or a drumstick or a toy clicker) and sends him to the backyard out of hearing distance. The father may have asked questions (why is it fun to ring the doorbell?), depending on age, etc. The father is using a full strategy — one that increases chances of generating a *normative* result from a child who is seen as a *full* child.

In many cases the FULL STRATEGY would be the hardest, and the EXCHANGE or COERCIVE STRATEGY, the easiest.

No matter what I tell you, the child will probably be back in a few days ringing the hell out of the doorbell, unless you've invented something the child can get to — like that toy clicker in the backyard — that's more fun.

DESCRIBE, PREDICT, EXPLAIN

What I've said above is the outline of a simple theory, and at best theories help *describe, predict,* and *explain.* I hope the above might help you *describe* various child behaviors like a disagreement about bedtime, or no dessert, or...you'll be able to start naming examples. And I believe it can help you *predict* what might happen in certain situations — how a certain father behavior (coercion, for example) might tend to generate a certain child behavior or attitude (alienation), and how client and calculative attitudes might form a bridge from coercive and alienated attitudes toward full child and normative attitudes. I think my Simple Theory can help you *explain* to yourself or someone else, your spouse, for example, about how simple coercion, without regard to other factors, might foreshadow a Factor Bad — as a consequence of how the child is seen.

Test:

Q. A child seen as a client is talking to a child who sees himself as alienated. The client child says, "Has your father ever used, to your knowledge, any exchange strategies?" What does the other child say?

A. "What kind of book have you been reading?"

How to Avoid Factor Bads

RELAXATION, INVOLVEMENT

If you're easily disturbed, try to lie back and accept some inconsequential things that are not easy for you to accept. Use your earplugs. Go ahead and let your child go barefoot on a cold day.

If you're way laid-back, you might want to get a bit more involved, get in tune with some ways to prevent bad behaviors through a relationship with your child that calls for talk and listening and reasonable firmness. This is best started very early in the child's life.

But your job is of course not just preventing bad behaviors. Another part, down the line and as soon as possible, is generating norms of, for example, fair play and moderation that your kids buy into.

PREDICTABILITY, COMPOSURE

As much as possible kids need to be warned of any upcoming time-out or behavior consequences so that the structure you are providing — rewards, suggestions, rules — falls into a pattern children understand clearly. This means that if you're in a bad mood and they are annoying you, you don't fly off the handle if you can help it. If you can walk away before losing your temper, that's a good strategy. But if you do fly off the handle, and scream, it's a good idea to apologize and explain what happened as best you can—talk about what happened and why (but, please, not in some guilt-ridden *long* explanation). You don't want to be the bearer of painful lightning that strikes out of nowhere and scares the hell out of a child. Because we believe we understand them thoroughly, we sometimes overlook the fact that they can be very fragile.

PLAY

Earlier I mentioned how important it is to spend a lot of time playing with your kid, on the floor, in the yard, in the woods, on the couch, wherever you can, wrestling, playing tag or ride-a-little-horsey-down-to-town. If you do all this and laugh with your kid, then firm and just behavior management is a much more readily available option for you. Though jumping from a playmate role to a cop role can be tricky—a good policy is simplicity and clarity and not too much explaining when they are very little.

On the other hand, "play" may not be your style. I'm sure that doesn't mean the end of the world. You can perhaps make your second toe cross over your big toe or snap your earlobe and do finger tricks. As long as you're *there*. You are, or are about to be, involved in a mammoth art project—the making and molding of a new life.

If you just show up once in a while to limit your child's

behavior, the child may often think of you as an asshole, and it's going to be hard to establish a solid, healthy relationship.

REWARD, PUNISHMENT, AND ANGER

I've tried all sorts of reward systems ("Consistency is the hobgoblin of little minds"...or was that "a foolish consistency"?), and yes, I know *punishment* is a bad word in many psychobabble circles. But I wasn't born yesterday. I believe language is, in most cases, the surface of an iceberg that may or may not be dangerous.

A recent reward system Kristina and I tried, and it worked fairly well, goes like this. A chart has the children's names and a column for mark-ups and a column for mark-downs. If a child shows unusually positive behavior, he or she gets a mark-up. Unusually negative behavior brings mark-downs. A mark-up cancels a mark-down. At the end of two-weeks, the child with the fewest mark-downs (or the most mark-ups) gets taken alone to a movie with a parent. The child with the most mark-downs loses one day of "screen time" for every mark-down in excess of the next highest number. It's important to warn a child that if a certain behavior continues, it might result in a mark-down. I've kept this description general to accommodate various family living styles, values, and the ages of the children. You may need to develop a system that is different. Our newest system involves daily chores split three ways—without mark-ups or mark-downs.

I think asking the child questions, exploring your rationale for any punishment/reward system, and then getting his

"I'm sorry son, but according to the chart you're grounded for the next ten years."

feedback is a good idea. I find that our children's proposed systems of rewards and punishments (revealed in discussions and family meetings) are often more punitive than ours.

From the time the child is five or six months old till about three years old, I think you need to be relatively directive, without too much discussion and rationale stated to the child. "Today we're going to pick up the toys in the backyard together. They should not be left out in the storm that's on the way. Let's go." Or "Please pick up the toys in the yard because it's about to rain." As you sense a child is beginning to reason through actions and understand concepts of fairness, it's probably a good idea to consider more talking, discussion, listening.

Your kids may hate you once in a while—and tell you—but I hope they are never afraid of you, of your anger.

If your wife is against spanking, I think that should end any discussion. If you and your wife are deciding whether or not to spank, I'd say no, don't do it.

However, because I was spanked (not beaten with a belt like some of my friends) and have on occasion spanked each of my children, and because some of you are for it and some against (I'm writing with a large audience in mind), I will not avoid the issue and will suggest how to *not* spank.

1. Never spank in anger. This is difficult—and important. If you're angry, walk away—no matter what. Your anger may result from a kind of fusion with your child. Sometimes we see our children as a part of ourselves, like a hand, and if the hand won't do as we say, or continues to do what we tell it not to do, we may become afraid (though the fear is already translated into anger by the time we catch up with it). Much anger is based on a fear that can be dismantled through thinking through what we're afraid of.

2. Don't spank without warning ("I'm going to count to three and if you don't come, you'll get a spanking"), and the kid should be old enough to be clear about any instructions they willfully disobey.

3. Don't spank on bare skin or slap a bare hand.

I'll add that if spanking becomes a habit, that's probably not good, because of what your child is learning about how to solve problems.

If you, down the line, find yourself feeling a bit helpless in the face of your children's ignoring you, and you're trying to "reason" with them and avoid spanking but things don't seem to be going well, then read this book: John Rosemond's *The New! Six-Point Plan for Raising Happy, Healthy Children*. Rosemond here avoids the topic of spanking and offers some sensible approaches to handling behavior problems. I wish I'd read this book before I ever spanked a child. Spanking would have then seemed unnecessary. Rosemond scoffs at, I might add, the "one minute for one year of age" time-out rule. Your reading such a book should happen in the context of your understanding that "behavior problems" are probably most directly related to the *relationship* between parents and children and may have a hell of a lot to do with the behavior of the parents, of you. Much of this is not as simple as many writers (including Rosemond — and me) sometimes seem to indicate.

Managing your anger so that your child is not afraid of you doesn't mean you shouldn't get angry or alarmed about certain behaviors. When I find myself about to blow up, I often press an imaginary button between my eyes that starts a clock running backwards for ten seconds. I count to myself, and then mentally play a scene from Cormac McCarthy's *Outer Dark,* where a guy is trying to buy cheese and crackers from a store clerk and the back-and-forth conversation becomes absurd. I'm sometimes able to inwardly laugh and find peace.

If you consistently *don't* express anger at your children (appropriately), or ever talk about it, they may be less likely down the line to manage their own anger well. If you talk with them about your anger ("I got angry because..."), about their anger ("I can understand why you'd be angry about..."), and about how and when anger is appropriate, how it can be handled well and not so well, and *choices* that can be made, then your children may adjust to their world more successfully than otherwise. (But be careful about initiating serious, explanatory conversations before your child is old enough to understand. She won't be interested in listening.) And as they learn to understand, you should perhaps occasionally talk about love, and sorrow, and reverence, and anxiety — but again, be sure the child is old enough to understand and join in the conversation while you listen.

There will be times when your children don't want to talk to you, and in some cases those may be good times to leave them alone.

If you are ever unfair or scary in your anger, then, again, I suggest you apologize. You may discover yourself saying something like "If you get really angry at somebody smaller than you and scare him or her, you need to apologize and try not to do that again because it's wrong." But those words, any words, will have less power than your actions, past and future. Your actions set a standard for your child's view of right and wrong in the world — and your actions include your questions, your words of explanation, guidance, empathy, and apologies.

You will not make your children better human beings by screaming at them, belittling them, or putting them down. Doing that will increase the chances of their being that way toward others and thus having a hard time in the world. The rumble will come.

And if, at the other extreme, you strive to be "popular"

with your kids by going along with whatever they want, then you're probably increasing your and your spouse's chances of living with brats for the rest of your lives. They can't just do what they want to do — you'll have to restrict their freedom occasionally, maybe daily. How you implement restrictions will help determine your children's attitude about you — do they come to dislike *you?* Or is it that they respect you and like you, but dislike some of what you require of them?

If you and your wife can be together on these issues, you are lucky and your life will be easier. If the two of you don't see eye to eye, talk through as much as you can and understand how you can best work together. Children need to understand that their parents, while having different parenting styles, love each other and support each other's parenting. It's okay if the two of you see things from different angles, but very important that the children feel that you love each other and act on that love.

RESPECT

Respect means that you do not several times a day uniformly praise a child in general, but rather recognize her hard work when she finishes a difficult task or acts in a praiseworthy way that is more than expected. Praise the *act* that is praiseworthy — the behavior of the child. This helps create an even-headed (versus a big-headed) kid.

Respect means you allow her to explain her anger or hurt while you listen, and that you are willing to apologize for your own bad behavior. (Sometimes a child is willing to talk to a sock puppet rather than a parent, or through a banana telephone.)

MODELING BY VOLUNTEERING

A premise of this book is that the healthy flow of life through a child, a healthy flow that enables a child to become a child in full, is essential for happiness and fruitfulness. If such a healthy flow is generally available for children whose parents are well-off financially but not for the poor, then the dreams and ideals of democracy, national health, and community are compromised. I'm asking you to take a deep breath, find that hour or so a week, and consider volunteering in a school near you, if you're not already doing this. You can make a difference in the lives of students and teachers. And your child's seeing you volunteer will possibly change the direction of his or her life. Twice a year Caleb teaches junior high students how to jump-start an automobile, throw a cast net, and light a match in a thirty-knot wind.

Just this morning I took a banjo and a chicken into a class of kindergarten kids. The kids were of mixed economic background and race. The unity in their delight at seeing and hearing a banjo and watching me put a chicken to sleep was dramatic. It's hard to look into those faces and believe that by the time they complete or drop out of high school, some will probably be leading broken and sad lives.

Speaking of volunteering, nursing homes are dry places that need the humidity of visits from children. Most residents will find rare delight in the presence of a child. Just walk in with a child and see what happens.

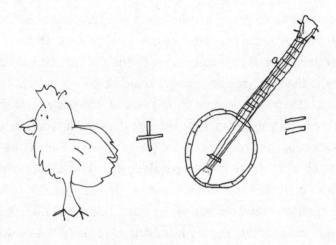

FINALLY

If you come to believe your teenagers are never going to speak to you again as long as you live—and they may tell you this—then you will be relieved. No, seriously, while they may tell you that, chances are that by their early twenties they will come around the bend and you'll be able to talk and laugh with them again. And rebuild the trust that was always beneath the surface. Even if they once rumbled on the lawn. No matter *what* happens in high school, try to remember that chances are good that things will turn out okay. When you find yourself at the end of the rope, don't turn it loose.

Raising a kid is not a method, or a system, nor does it come from some proven "technique." It's art. It calls for an occasional, if not a frequent, embracing of uncertainty. It's an art that depends on the manipulation, balancing, and juggling of three factors—your experience, your observation, and your imagination, toolboxes from which you can draw fathering tools. Every day for about eighteen years you will be making decisions that require you to work through a knotted mass of information, emotion, and intuition. Much of the time you may be saying, I could have done better.

So it's okay to read up on fatherhood, but you've also got 1) your own experience in the world to guide you—stuff that's happened to you as a kid (or an adult) when you were treated unfairly or were particularly thankful about someone's attitude toward you. And you've got 2) your observation—all that you've seen and heard and read. And then, importantly, 3) your imagination suggests the future, helps you see where to take a chance, a big chance or a little chance, or to not take a chance at all. You may have a lot going for you, already. You know that parenting is less about what you do to a child than about what you do with a child.

PART FIVE

GETTING FIXED

(FOR FATHERS ONLY, PLEASE)

My four children bring me happiness and joy. I am blessed with happiness and joy and children. So, several years ago, not long after the last child was born, Kristina and I decided that I'd get a vasectomy.

The preparation information and instructions I brought home from the doctor included orders to shave my scrotum — no more than twenty-four hours before the operation. My appointment was for two o'clock on a Thursday, and somehow I'd put off the shaving until just before one thirty. I wasn't about to shave early and go in there with a five o'clock shadow.

I didn't want to use an electric razor — my electric razor, anyway. It tends to pull. I needed a disposable razor. I asked my wife if she had one.

"Single blade or double?" she asked.

"Double, I guess."

I stood naked in the bathroom, holding the razor in one hand and a can of her shaving cream in the other. I looked around. Tub should work.

I decided the best thing to do would be to sit on the edge of the tub with my feet in, turn on the faucet (it was to my right), lather up, and proceed. But when I got situated, I realized that my position wasn't quite working, so I straddled the tub wall, faced the faucet, and shifted to the left so I could get at the job more easily. (Aunt Myrtle, I labeled this section "For fathers only.")

I splashed on warm water and lathered up. Remember, I'm just after the scrotum, no more. The lathering up was no problem at all. Plenty of lather. I took razor in hand and was trying to remember if a razor was supposed to go against the grain or with. I was then wondering which way the grain *was,* when in wandered Nathaniel, my then three-year-old son.

"What you doing, Daddy?"

"Oh, just getting ready to go to the doctor."

"What are you doing?"

"I'm just...going to shave. I need some privacy."

"What is all that white stuff?"

"That's shaving cream. I'm shaving."

"Why?"

"I just am. I'll be out in a minute. You wait for me in the living room, or somewhere."

He walked out.

So. I reached down and sort of stretched the skin as I do when shaving my face with a razor, and started in, but a major problem was that I couldn't see down there. I bent over some, shifted to the left a little more. Wups. Almost lost my balance.

What about a handheld mirror? Humm, everything would be backwards. But it was backwards when I shaved my face, wasn't it? In this present case, though, I'd be looking *down* into the mirror at something above...and also, it would be backwards, a reflection. My mind flashed to that phrase,

"Objects in mirror are closer than they appear." Or was it "smaller than you think"?

I decided to forgo the mirror and proceed by feel. Slowly. I shaved a swath.

I wondered: if I stood and bent way over...could I see better? But I am not flexible. My wife can flatten her hands on the floor while standing.

"Honey?" I called.

"Yes."

"...Nothing."

"How's it going?" she asked. "It's almost time to leave." She was not reluctant for me to get on with this procedure.

"Oh, it's going fine."

And the procedure did go fine. But I'm going to miss babies in the house—the great fun part of it all, the new knowledge of the world through their eyes and through their words. Being a father is perhaps more important than anything else you and I will ever do. It's one important way we live beyond our lifetime. For some of us it may be hard to realize that a genuine relationship with our child needs to be formed early and nurtured with everything our experience, observation, and imagination can muster, and that that calls for listening, and answering questions, and long talks, and hugging, and setting limits, and loving. Maybe one of the best ways to be a good father is to be a good mother—and to teach that to our sons and daughters.

ACKNOWLEDGMENTS

Thanks to Liz Darhansoff, Pat Strachan, Ben George, Donna Levine, Ben Allen, Sterling Hennis, Dee Perry, Phillip Schlechty, George Singleton, George Terll, Uncle Bob, Ernest and Truma Edgerton, Eric Porterfield, Susan Ketchin, John and Barbara Penick, David and Nancy McGirt, Mason Williams, Susan H. McDaniel, my children—Catherine, Nathaniel, Ridley, and Truma, who bring me fresh life daily—and especially to Kristina.

"Them Toad Suckers" was published in a wonderful book for all human beings, *The Mason Williams Reading Matter*, Doubleday and Company Inc. © 1969. Cited with permission of Mason Williams.

ABOUT THE AUTHOR

Clyde Edgerton was born in Durham, North Carolina. He is the author of a memoir and ten novels, including *Walking Across Egypt, Lunch at the Piccadilly, The Bible Salesman,* and *The Night Train.* He has been a Guggenheim Fellow and is a member of the Fellowship of Southern Writers. Edgerton teaches creative writing at the University of North Carolina Wilmington. He lives in Wilmington with his wife, Kristina, and their children.

ABOUT THE ILLUSTRATOR

Daniel Wallace is the author of five novels, including *Big Fish* and *The Kings and Queens of Roam.* He has illustrated books by George Singleton and Marianne Gingher, and his drawings and cartoons have appeared in magazines all over the place. He lives in Chapel Hill with his wife, Laura Kellison Wallace, where he directs the creative writing program at the University of North Carolina.

Also by Clyde Edgerton

The Night Train
A novel

"*The Night Train* is a poignant depiction of a small community on the edge of irreversible change....So many novelists strive to capture the times that shape the rest of someone's life. Most of them fail. A novel containing moments like this is nothing less than a gift."   —Kevin O'Kelly, *Boston Globe*

"Future historians can study Edgerton's body of work for what he does best: capturing that elusive sense of place and people in the context of a twentieth-century era....Edgerton's genius is his ability to capture the nuances of small-town life....Like Charles Dickens, Edgerton is a comic novelist of serious subjects who floats from character to character."

—John McNally, *Washington Post*

"Mr. Edgerton brings a sure hand to depicting Dwayne and Larry Lime's friendship....He achieves a sweet sense of triumph...when the boys' secret musical alliance spectacularly—and soulfully—breaks into the open."

—Sam Sacks, *Wall Street Journal*

Back Bay Books • Available wherever books are sold

Also by Clyde Edgerton

The Bible Salesman

A novel

"How good it feels to throw back one's head and howl with a great comic novel. The 'burial tuck' alone should make *The Bible Salesman* a classic."　　　　　—David Sedaris

"Achingly poignant and ripsnortingly funny....*The Bible Salesman* is so sweet and funny that its darker themes sneak up quietly on the reader."

　　　　　—J. Peder Zane, *Raleigh News & Observer*

"Reminiscent not so much of Faulkner or Flannery O'Connor as of Charles Dickens's *The Pickwick Papers*....There are immense pleasures in the tales patched together in *The Bible Salesman*."　　　　　—John McNally, *Washington Post*

"A deeply satisfying novel, and great fun....Clyde Edgerton's storytelling is sublime."

　　　　　—Harriett Roberson, *Charleston Post and Courier*

Back Bay Books • Available wherever books are sold